vegetarian party food

celia brooks brown

vegetarian party food

photography by Jan Baldwin

PAVILION

contents

foreword

"A vegetarian is not a person who lives on vegetables, any more than a Catholic is a person who lives on cats." – George Bernard Shaw

There are all sorts of reasons for giving up or cutting down on meat. For me, meat is something that has just never been appealing. I was 19 when I moved to Britain from the US in 1989, and back then I ate chicken occasionally, but I'd never eaten much other meat. I was no gourmet – I lived on packet soup, salads and fast food. Boiling a kettle and opening packets was the extent of my culinary skills. Not long after I arrived, there was a food scare in Britain. It put me off chicken, and I gave up meat for good.

Soon after giving up meat, I started to develop an interest in cooking. This is no coincidence. I knew I couldn't live on cans of beans and lumps of fatty cheese. As my mental perception of food became more acute – I started to see food as something other than just fuel – my sensory perception improved too. I was desperate to learn how to cook, so I could explore the creative process of using ingredients, tools and all five senses to make something delicious. The greatest satisfaction of all, I found, was giving other people pleasure through eating what I prepared. I soon discovered that food that is cooked with passion evokes passion in the person eating it.

The whole realm of food is a healthy obsession for me, and it's not limited to cooking. So much of the fun and fascination lies in shopping for fresh, high-quality ingredients in farmers' markets and specialist food shops. It also includes poring over heaps of books about food and filling my head with recipes, folklore, culinary and social history. I'm also rather partial to stuffing my face.

My passion became a career in vegetarian cooking, through catering, teaching and writing. I'm certainly no vegetarian "evangelist". I merely hope to show people how easy and fun it can be to cook, and meat is simply not part of my repertoire. You must have what I call a "sensory relationship" with what you cook. If you can't engage every sense with your ingredients, what you cook just won't taste right. Even if I were to go through the mechanics of cooking a piece of meat, it would probably taste horrible.

My approach, in a nutshell, is this: vegetarian cooking is more complex than simply slapping something on the grill. It requires more thought, more construction. If you're not used to vegetarian cooking, try to think beyond the "meat and two veg" convention, where vegetables play second fiddle. Try to create a balance of textures, colours and flavours, and no one will notice the absence of meat.

Finally, when I tell people I'm vegetarian, the question that often follows is, "Do you eat fish?" OK, so vegetarians who eat fish are not technically vegetarians, but since when has the enjoyment of food been a technical business? I don't see it as "hypocrisy" to eat a bit of fish. People should be allowed to make their own decisions about what they put in their bodies and why. (That includes meat-eaters.) This modern breed of "pescetarians" are not rare, so I've included some fish recipes here for them, having done my best to recommend fish that is as eco-friendly as possible. This book is for every food lover, vegetarian or not. I hope you savour every page.

Celia Brooks Brown

how to use this book

These days what you decide to cook is as much determined by the event — a casual brunch party, a swanky cocktail evening — as the time of year. So, I've grouped the recipes by the occasions they lend themselves to. At the beginning of each chapter are some general advice and organizational tips, while in the middle I have suggested a menu for the occasion and given advice on planning, crockery and drinks. All the recipes are designed for you to create a menu for everyone to enjoy, not just vegetarians, and I hope that some of the dishes will become part of your daily repertoire as well.

plan ahead — the golden rules of entertaining

Rule 1   **A strong menu is the foundation of success:**

Design a menu that's convenient to prepare in the available time.

Stick to seasonal ingredients.

Balance the colour, flavour and texture of every part of the meal.

Determine your budget — you can be generous without spending a fortune.

Think outside the starter-main-dessert box. Consider serving several small courses, or canapés followed by a humdinger of a course.

Consider the weather and how it affects what you want to eat — for example, cold soup on a hot day is magic.

Provide a little something to eat with alcoholic drinks, even if it's as simple as a bowl of nuts or olives.

Rule 2   **Make life easy for yourself wherever possible:**

Consider hiring plates, cutlery, even tables and chairs. Events hire companies will usually let you send everything back dirty for a small charge.

Consider your entertaining space — people inevitably gravitate to the kitchen at parties, but try to let the party actually happen well away from the working space.

Clean out your fridge. You can never have too much fridge space. Borrow fridge space at your neighbour's — as long as you invite them! For a big do, hire a fridge.

Get your shopping out of the way the day before you start cooking.

Rope in as much human help as possible. Appoint or hire one helper per 10 guests.

If you've got lots of kids coming, provide a different menu for them, but for heaven's sake, don't knock yourself out cooking! Provide them with the stuff they'll like: chips, pizzas and fun sweets in individual packets as well as some of the grown-up food.

If you are heating or cooking kids' food, don't forget to factor that in to oven and fridge space.

Rule 3

Remember the mundane but crucial details:

Get a big rubbish (trash) bin sorted out. Buy plenty of bin (trash) bags.

More and more people seem to have food intolerances these days. It is their responsibility to tell you ahead of time if they have special requirements. If they tell you once they've arrived and there's nothing for them to eat, don't feel bad – let them raid the kitchen.

Don't forget paper napkins – little ones for canapés, large ones for everything else, and at least two per person.

If it's cold outside, decide where people can put their coats.

bar basics

If you're the cook, nominate someone else to be in charge of the bar.

Rough quantities of wine: allow half a bottle of white wine and half a bottle of red per person. If it's bubbly all night, allow three quarters of a bottle per person.

If you can get it "sale or return" from your wine merchant, opt for more.

Open (non-sparkling) wine and replace the corks before people arrive.

Save wine boxes for empty bottles. Recycle.

Consider hiring glasses. Many booze shops offer free glass hire, provided you send them back clean. Some will inevitably break. For a big do, hire twice as many wine glasses as guests. People have one drink, put their glass down, then when they're ready for another, they forget where they put it or it's been cleared away, so they'll be needing another.

Provide tumblers as well as wine glasses for soft drinks and cocktails.

Get one pillow-sized bag of ice (about 11kg/25lbs for every 10 people).

Call an ice company who will deliver. Start chilling drinks at least two hours before kick-off.

Drinks chill faster in an ice bath (ice plus water) than "on-ice" or in the fridge.

Don't clog your fridge with booze. Fill big tubs or your bathtub with ice and water.

Provide lots of sparkling and still mineral water.

For a big do, don't offer too many different drinks. Stick with wine and beer, or one fabulous cocktail.

Keep the soft drinks simple. Provide a cordial such as elderflower or a jug (pitcher) of thawed concentrated juice for mixing with mineral water.

shopping & storage strategies

Make space in your fridge and in the kitchen for your ingredients before you shop.

Think quality. Buy the best of everything you can get.

If you come across a real bargain, you might consider altering the menu – but only if it's a fresh, high-quality ingredient. For instance, don't buy two-for-one strawberry punnets if they're looking a bit off!

Organic food is usually superior, but it's more perishable. Inspect fresh produce carefully and use as soon as possible. Washed root vegetables will perish faster.

Organic eggs are always superior. Store in the fridge.

Local ethnic groceries are treasure troves and can be an inspirational source of raw ingredients and special sweets or savouries.

Support small businesses. Buy local produce where possible.

Salad leaves and fresh herbs should be purchased no earlier than a day before your party.

Spray lettuces with water and store in the fridge, away from the fridge walls to avoid "fridge burn".

Bunches of fresh herbs should be washed and kept in a vase of water.

Never refrigerate basil or tomatoes. Keep berries in the fridge.

Take all fruit and vegetables out of any plastic wrapping.

health matters

When you're entertaining, it's time to live a little. Indulgence is a good thing, in moderation. The fact is, healthy food makes you feel good – it boosts energy levels, strength and vitality. On a day-to-day basis, everyone benefits from a healthy diet – roughly, that means low fat, lots of complex carbohydrates (like whole grains), fibre, a little protein and plenty of fresh fruit and veg. I think the occasional naughty nibble is also essential for good cheer.

a vegetarian diet is a model diet

Research has shown that a vegetarian diet improves health, which is a great reason to eat vegetarian food occasionally or always. Vegetarians need to replace the nutrients meat contains, in particular protein, iron, B vitamins and selenium. Sources of these nutrients are abundant in an ideal vegetarian diet, which consists of a variety of foods including grains, beans, pulses, fruit, vegetables, nuts or seeds, and a small amount of fat. It's best not to rely on cheese as a source of protein – animal fat is saturated fat – though low-fat dairy products like yoghurt are an important source of calcium. Eggs are packed with essential nutrients, but should also be eaten in moderation.

the entertainer's bag of tricks — Following is a list of handy ingredients to stock in the kitchen, so you're effortlessly prepared to cook with confidence, comfort and finesse.

flavours for salty seasoning

Soy sauce – dark (fermented), light (unfermented)

Thai fish sauce – (nam pla)

Worcestershire sauce – traditional or vegetarian

Stock – high-quality vegetable stock powder or cubes

flavours for heat & spice

Chilli – fresh (store in freezer indefinitely or fridge until crinkly), dried (smoked and non), cayenne pepper, mild chilli powder; chilli sauces: Thai sweet chilli, Tabasco, Jamaican hot; pickled chillies (sliced jalapeños, whole varieties); smoked Spanish paprika (pimentón)

Whole spices – black mustard seeds, pink peppercorns, fennel seeds, cumin seeds, coriander seeds, cardamom, fenugreek, saffron strands, whole nutmegs, cinnamon sticks, vanilla pods

flavours for depth, body & accent

Oils & vinegars – extra virgin olive, sesame, truffle and walnut oils; aged balsamic and rice vinegars

Booze for cooking – Madeira, sherry, vermouth (substitute for white wine), mirin (Japanese cooking wine), port, brandy or Cognac, rum

Fresh herbs – flat-leaf parsely, basil, mint, sage, bay, coriander (cilantro)

flavours for a sweet tooth

Honey, golden (pouring) syrup, molasses, malt extract, rose water, orange blossom water, lemon curd

Pure cocoa powder (unsweetened cocoa), 70 per cent cocoa solids plain (semisweet) chocolate, white chocolate

tasty morsels

Assorted olives, capers in vinegar or salt, caperberries, sun-dried or semi-dried tomatoes in oil (semi-dried usually store in the fridge), artichoke hearts in oil, pickled onions, pickled baby beetroot (beet), cornichons and pickled cucumbers, dried porcini (cèpes) mushrooms, dried shiitake mushrooms, canned stuffed vine leaves, canned houmous

Nuts – (all shelled) pine nuts, peanuts, vacuum-packed chestnuts, hazelnuts, walnuts, pecans, pistachios, cashews; almonds: whole blanched, flaked, slivered, ground; peanut butter

Seeds – (all hulled) sesame seeds, poppy seeds, pumpkin seeds, hemp seeds,

Dried fruits – sultanas (golden raisins), raisins, apricots, prunes, cranberries, figs, coconut

staples

Noodles and pasta – egg, rice, soba and vermicelli noodles; linguine, shapes and orzo pasta

Rice and other grains – basmati, risotto, wholegrain and long-grain rice; couscous, bulgur wheat and quinoa grains

Legumes and tinned vegetables – lentils, dried beans, canned beans of all sorts, including refried beans; artichoke hearts, roasted (bell) peppers, hearts of palm, roasted green chillies, water chestnuts

freezer essentials

Chopped and leaf spinach, peas, frozen berries, pastry, ice cream, kaffir lime leaves and lemon grass, chillies, bread such as Turkish flatbread, tortillas, vodka, ice

1

canapés & cocktail bites

simple little bites with minimum fiddle, to serve with drinks

Canapé is derived from a French word meaning "sofa" — a tasty morsel reclining on an edible cushion before being popped in the mouth. The word has come to encompass all party nibbles – something tiny but delicious, to indulge the taste buds and buffer the effects of alcohol.

There's no doubt that hot, crispy fried stuff is usually the most popular food to accompany drinks, but only if it's served as soon as it's fried. This means the cook is stuck in the kitchen, and the grease is stuck to the cook (and the cook's fancy outfit). If you're still up for it, visit the freezer department of an Asian market and you'll find tasty vegetarian spring rolls, dim sum and wontons (read the labels to double check for any sneaky meat ingredients). Sink them into hot oil until golden, then serve with chilli sauce.

If you're the cook and the host, however, rely on your pal the oven to do the cooking while you see to other things. It's a good idea to carry a small kitchen timer with you if you leave things in the oven while the guests arrive. The smell of burnt food is distinctive and embarrassing. Believe me, I've done it more than once.

The selection of canapés you choose should be a logical balance of hot and cold, and low on last-minute labour. Here are my guidelines on quantity (per head):

Pre-lunch canapés: 2–3 different canapés, 1–2 of each
Canapés as an appetizer: 3 different canapés, 1–2 of each
Early evening canapé party: 6–8 different canapés, 1–2 of each
Canapés instead of the evening meal: 8 different canapés, 2–3 of each
Stick to the smaller quantity when providing canapés that are larger than one bite.

cucumber & herbed mascarpone bites

Here, the quintessentially English cucumber sandwich gets dressed up in a modern style, and nibbled out of a carved bread bowl. Make up to four hours in advance.

ingredients

makes 36

1 large, round, rustic loaf of bread

250g/9oz mascarpone cheese

4 heaped tablespoons finely chopped fresh herbs, such as dill, parsley, tarragon and chives

grated zest of 1 lemon

salt and freshly ground black pepper

2–3 shakes Tabasco sauce

8 slices wholemeal (whole-wheat) square sandwich bread

½ cucumber, sliced paper-thin

method

To make the container, cut a circle out of the top of the loaf, leaving a border around the edge. Hollow out to form a "bread bowl", then cover with cling film (plastic wrap) until ready to use.

Beat together the mascarpone cheese, herbs, lemon zest, salt, pepper and Tabasco sauce, then spread evenly over 2 slices of bread. Place a layer of cucumber slices over the mixture on 1 slice, then top with the other slice of bread. Slice off the crusts, then cut each sandwich into 9 little squares. Repeat with the remaining ingredients.

Fill the bread bowl with the sandwich bites, cover with cling film (plastic wrap) and keep in the refrigerator until ready to serve. (You may have enough bites to refill the bowl.)

spice-crusted baby potatoes with tamarind cream

These tiny spuds, studded with crunchy spices, always go down a treat. The dip has an element of surprise – the tamarind – that really gets people talking. Cherry-sized potatoes are ideal, so they can just be popped in the mouth.

ingredients

serves 20 as part of a canapé menu, 8–10 as finger food

1kg/2lb 4oz baby new potatoes, scrubbed
1 tablespoon coriander seeds
1 tablespoon cumin seeds
1/2 teaspoon ground turmeric
1/2 teaspoon cayenne pepper
1 teaspoon celery salt or sea salt
3 tablespoons olive oil
1 tablespoon wine vinegar

for the tamarind cream

100ml/scant 1/2 cup crème fraîche
    or soured cream
100ml/scant 1/2 cup natural (plain) yoghurt
2 tablespoons prepared tamarind, diluted if thick to
    dribbling consistency (see Top Tip below)

method

Preheat the oven to 220°C/425°F/Gas 7. Par-boil the potatoes in enough well salted water to cover for 5 minutes, then drain and leave to cool. Dry them with a clean cloth.

Grind the coriander and cumin seeds in a mortar or spice grinder, then mix with the remaining spices and salt. Whisk together the oil, vinegar and spices in a bowl. Place the potatoes on a large baking sheet, then pour over the oil mixture and toss well to coat evenly. Roast them in the oven for about 15–20 minutes, until tender. Use tongs to remove the potatoes from the baking sheet and set aside until required. Reserve the toasted spices left on the baking sheet.

For the tamarind cream, beat together the crème fraîche or soured cream and yoghurt, then stir in the reserved spices. Scrape the cream mixture into a bowl and dribble over the tamarind. Serve with warm or cold potatoes. Use cocktail sticks (toothpicks) if desired.

top tip

To prepare tamarind from pulp, soak a hunk in boiling water to liquify, then press through a sieve (see photos above).

cranberry filo (phyllo) cigars

Sweet and sour cranberries combined with almonds, capers and spice give these crispy nibbles an intriguing flavour. Is it sweet or is it savoury? People have fun trying to guess just what goes into these Middle-Eastern inspired pastries.

ingredients

makes about 15

55g/¹/₂ cup dried cranberries

55g/¹/₂ cup ground almonds

1 tablespoon capers in vinegar, drained

1 tablespoon fresh oregano or marjoram, leaves stripped

¹/₂ teaspoon cumin seeds

4 small sheets filo (phyllo) pastry (approximately 16 x 30cm/6¹/₄ x 12in)

2 tablespoons butter, melted

method

Preheat the oven to 220°C/425°F/Gas 7. Place the cranberries in a bowl and pour over enough boiling water to cover. Leave to soak for 15–20 minutes, or until soft, then drain thoroughly. Place the reconstituted cranberries, ground almonds, capers, oregano or marjoram and cumin seeds in a food processor or spice grinder and process until a purée results. Alternatively, chop everything very small and combine thoroughly.

Lightly grease a baking sheet and line with baking paper (parchment paper). Lay 1 sheet of filo (phyllo) pastry out horizontally on a clean, flat surface and brush all over with melted butter. Keep the rest of the pastry sheets covered with a damp towel. Along the bottom of the pastry, about 2cm/³/₄in above the edge, arrange a long strip of the filling, about a pencil's width. Fold the bottom edge carefully over the filling, then roll the entire long sausage up tightly, moving along in sections, until rolled into 1 long cigar.

Using a knife or kitchen scissors, snip off the very ends of the cigar, then snip into baby cigars, about 5cm/2in long. Place on the baking sheet and brush generously with butter. Repeat with the remaining pastry.

Bake the cigars in the preheated oven for about 10–15 minutes, until golden all over. Serve warm or cold.

think ahead

Make the cigars up to the stage before cutting and baking a day in advance. Keep in the refrigerator, covered and not touching each other.

top tip

Vegans can use olive oil in place of butter. When serving, these cigars have a habit of sliding around on the plate, so they're best served on a bamboo mat or from a bowl.

aubergine (eggplant), feta & mint skewers

Chargrilled aubergines (eggplants) look great dressed in black stripes – but you could oven-grill (broil) them instead. Assemble the skewers up to 4 hours in advance.

ingredients

makes 20

1 long, thin aubergine (eggplant), sliced as thinly as possible lengthways into 10 slices

olive oil, for brushing

100g/3½oz feta cheese, cut into approximately 20 x 1cm/¾in cubes

20 large fresh mint leaves

freshly ground black pepper

pomegranate molasses (page 71) or vintage balsamic vinegar, for drizzling

method

Place a ridged griddle pan (grill pan) over a high heat for 5 minutes or until very hot. Brush the aubergine (eggplant) slices with olive oil, then chargrill on both sides until translucent and striped with black. Leave to cool, then cut each slice into 2 long strips. Take 1 strip at a time and place a mint leaf on top, then tightly wrap both around a piece of feta. Secure with a bamboo skewer or cocktail stick and place on a large serving plate. Season to taste with black pepper, then drizzle with a little pomegranate molasses or a few drops of balsamic vinegar.

cranberry filo (phyllo) cigars (right), aubergine (eggplant), feta & mint skewers (left)

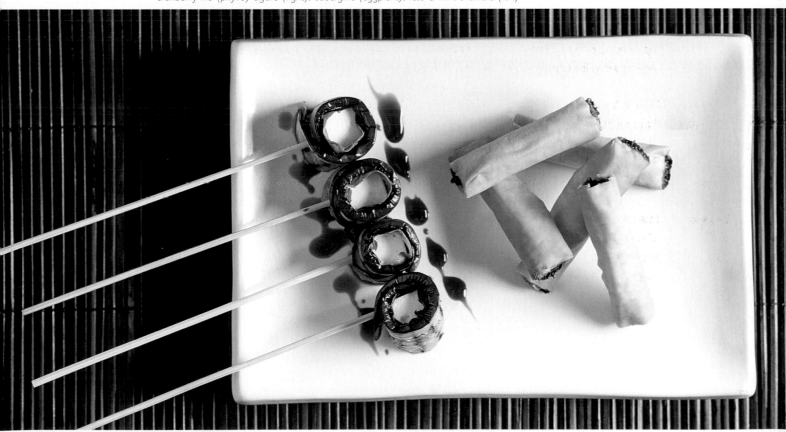

a cocktail bash —

Cocktail parties have a sparky energy — people are usually standing and committed to communicating, so they often drink more quickly than usual. Consequently, it's important to keep the food flowing as well as the drink, but do try to pace it over the evening. If you're busy in the kitchen, nominate friends or family members to circulate with your creations, explaining exactly what's in each one in case guests ask. Don't fuss around with too many garnishes — let the food speak for itself. Keep each canapé small, tidy and ideally one-bite size. Provide receptacles for used cocktail sticks, olive stones (pits), empty shot glasses, etc., and don't send hot food out too hot.

shopping   Asian markets are always worth a visit for party paraphernalia like cocktail sticks, funky napkins, serving dishes and glasses, candles, nuts and nibbles.

crockery   For serving canapés use plates, bowls, lacquer trays and bamboo steamer baskets. Assemble canapés on kitchen trays, then transfer to the serving dishes. Don't put too many canapés on at once: nobody ever wants the last, lone canapé.

drinks   The best way to get a party going is for the host to serve one strong cocktail to everyone as they arrive. Try:
champagne cocktail Place a sugar lump in the glass and shake on a few drops of Angostura bitters, then add a dash of brandy, and top up with champagne.
vodka martini Swirl vermouth in a glass, then discard to next. Top with ice-shaken or frozen neat vodka and an olive.

the menu

teriyaki almonds vegan

Shimmering clusters of glazed, toasted nuts are utterly irresistible. These are the ideal bar snack: salty, sweet and crunchy. You don't have to limit yourself to almonds – pecan nuts, cashews and Brazil nuts are all fantastic as well, though if you mix them, bear in mind they may not cook evenly.

ingredients

300g/scant 2 cups blanched whole almonds

3 tablespoons olive oil

2 tablespoons dark soy sauce

2 tablespoons mirin (Japanese cooking wine) or sweet sherry

$^1/_4$ teaspoon cayenne pepper

1 tablespoon sesame seeds

1 tablespoon caster (superfine) sugar

method

Preheat the oven to 200°C/400°F/Gas 6. Spread the almonds out on a baking sheet and toast in the preheated oven for 5 minutes, until pale golden. Lower the oven temperature to 150°C/300°F/Gas 2.

Combine the remaining ingredients in a bowl and mix well. Add the toasted almonds and stir to coat evenly. Pour the mixture back on to the baking sheet and cook in the oven for about 20–25 minutes, stirring every 5 minutes. The liquid will reduce in the oven, eventually becoming a thick, dark, sticky coating, which glazes the nuts.

Leave the nuts to cool on the baking sheet. Use a metal spatula to scrape the nuts and glaze off the sheet. Break up any large clumps, but leave some in little clusters. Arrange in a bowl and serve, with napkins nearby.

avocado & semi-dried tomato crostini vegan

The semi-dried tomato is the new sun-dried — it's softer, brighter and juicier — but good old sun-dried are fine too. The spicy avocado purée is best made no more than four hours before serving.

ingredients

makes 20

olive oil, for brushing

20 1cm/½in thick slices of very thin baguette
   or ciabatta

1 large or 2 small perfectly ripe avocados, peeled
   and stoned (pitted)

juice of 1 lime

1 garlic clove, crushed

1 teaspoon ground cumin

½ teaspoon hot chilli powder, or to taste

salt and freshly ground black pepper

20 pieces semi-dried tomato in oil, drained
   (or use sun-dried)

fresh chives, cut into 2cm/¾in lengths

method

To make the crostini, preheat the oven to 180°C/350°F/Gas 4. Brush a baking sheet with olive oil, then place the bread slices on the sheet and drizzle lightly with olive oil. Bake in the preheated oven for about 10 minutes, until light golden and thoroughly crisp. Leave to cool, then keep in an airtight container until ready to use.

To make the avocado purée, mash the avocado with a potato masher until smooth, then mash in the lime juice, garlic, cumin, chilli, salt and pepper. Cover with cling film (plastic wrap) and keep in the refrigerator until ready to use.

To assemble each canapé, place a small spoonful of avocado purée on each piece of bread. It looks prettiest if not smoothed down too much. Place a semi-dried tomato on top and finish with a piece of chive.

artichoke toasties (top), aubergine (eggplant) & olive truffles (bottom)

artichoke toasties

People can never seem to get enough of these warm, crisp and cheesy tartlets. They're ludicrously easy to make, so make more than you think you'll need. Using a posh loaf of bread for the bases is a waste of money and effort – regular white sandwich bread is the key to their simplicity.

ingredients

makes 24

12 slices medium-sliced white sandwich bread

soft butter, for spreading

400g/14oz can artichoke hearts, drained and chopped

55g/2oz fresh Parmesan cheese, finely grated

2 fresh, fleshy, mild green chillies, de-seeded and finely chopped

3 heaped tablespoons mayonnaise

a pinch of salt

freshly ground black pepper

method

Preheat the oven to 220°C/425°F/Gas 7. Using a 5cm/2in wide glass tumbler or biscuit cutter (cookie cutter), cut 2 circles of bread out of each slice. Butter one side fairly generously and press butter-side down in a shallow non-stick muffin tin, flattening the entire surface with your fingertips.

Mix together the remaining ingredients, then place a spoonful of the mixture into each bread case, smoothing down the top evenly. Bake in the preheated oven for 12–15 minutes, until golden and crisp. Leave to cool briefly before slipping out of the tin. Serve warm.

aubergine (eggplant) & olive truffles

These look rather like little meatballs, though they practically float off the plate with lightness. Try to serve them as soon as possible out of the oven – like most hot savouries, their appeal is immediate. Once let loose on the guests, they won't have a hope of hanging around. The mixture can be made up to one day in advance.

ingredients

makes 24

1 large aubergine (eggplant), approximately 500g/1lb 2oz
2 tablespoons olive oil
55g/¹/₂ cup pine nuts
20 kalamata olives, pitted and chopped
4 tablespoons dry breadcrumbs
6 tablespoons freshly grated Parmesan cheese, plus 2 tablespoons for sprinkling
2 tablespoons chopped fresh parsley
1 plump garlic clove, crushed
1 organic egg, beaten
butter, for greasing
to garnish (optional):
fresh parsley leaves
Parmesan cheese shavings

method

Preheat the oven to 230°C/450°F/Gas 8. Cut the aubergine (eggplant) in half lengthways and brush with olive oil. Roast in the preheated oven for about 30 minutes, until golden and completely soft. Leave to cool, then peel off the skin and discard, then chop the flesh finely. Lower the oven temperature to 200°C/400°F/Gas 6.

Mix the aubergine (eggplant) flesh, pine nuts, olives, breadcrumbs, Parmesan cheese, parsley, garlic and egg together in a bowl, then leave to rest for 10–15 minutes.

Liberally grease a large baking sheet. Form the mixture into bite-sized balls and place on the sheet, then top each one with a pinch of grated Parmesan cheese.

Bake in the oven for 15–20 minutes, until golden and puffed up. Serve hot, with a few parsley leaves and Parmesan shavings sprinkled over the platter, if desired.

feed the masses

big bowls and platters that go a long way, for finger and fork buffets

Cooking for a crowd usually means it's celebration time — a wedding,

a big birthday, a graduation. For these occasions, sandwiches just won't do! Food is the life of the party, and if you're the cook, it can seem a little daunting, but it's also huge fun and immensely satisfying. Don't rely on a "loaves and fishes" miracle; if you plan the menu sensibly and stay organized, everything will run as smooth as honey.

A stunning yet simple buffet is the best tactic for feeding crowds of people. Design a buffet with no more than four or five large dishes, which can be eaten standing, with a fork. They should have bold visual impact, presenting a contrast of textures, colours and flavours. Choose one or two delicious nibbles to keep people happy before the buffet begins, but avoid anything that's too fussy to make. Stick to one or two big desserts. Provide a back-up of a giant cheese and bread. Bear in mind that hungry people are greedy at buffets and may take more than their fair share.

The irony of feeding the masses is it takes almost the same amount of time to cook for 100 as it does for 1,000. Good food has to be fresh – so by nature it's ephemeral. The actual cooking can't be going on for much more than three days prior to the event. Solution? Delegation! Take on more pairs of hands than you think you need. Conserve energy and have the shopping delivered if you can. Sub-contract one of the desserts to a friend or a local bakery, and buy in things like petits-fours and tart cases.

Finally, as the marathon begins, start with a well-rested body. Make a list of every task that needs to be done and check them off as you go. Take plenty of breaks – get some fresh air. Top tip: drink water constantly, and don't forget to eat. You need to be firing on all cylinders!

Now, on your marks, get set...

tortellini skewers with herb oil

When cooking for large numbers, the smart entertainer will occasionally rely on a few bits which are prepared by the pros (or by machine) – and this is a good example. Those hours of labour making homemade tortellini can be put to much better use. Delicious fresh pasta is widely available in supermarkets, though if you can afford to be a little extravagant, get the tortellini made fresh at an Italian deli. These are perfect on a finger buffet; they're tempting, easy to eat and quite substantial.

ingredients

makes 24 skewers
48 cheese-filled tortellini
300g/10¹/₂oz mozzarella di bufala, *torn into coarse chunks*
24 high-quality pitted olives
12 sun-dried tomatoes in oil, each cut into 2 strips
for the oil:
approximately 20 fresh basil leaves
approximately 20 fresh flat-leaf parsley leaves
80ml/¹/₃ cup extra virgin olive oil

method

Wipe 24 bamboo skewers with a cloth to remove any splinters. Cook the tortellini in plenty of well salted boiling water until al dente. Drain, then rinse under delicately flowing cold water and spread out on a clean tea towel (dishtowel) to dry.

Pair up a piece of cheese with an olive and wrap a strip of sun-dried tomato around them. Thread 1 tortellini on to a bamboo skewer, followed by the tomato-cheese-olive wrap, and finishing with a tortellini close to the end of the skewer. (If you're feeling lazy or rushed, thread them on as haphazardly as you like – they'll still taste scrumptious.) Keep the finished skewers covered in cling film (plastic wrap) and leave to chill in the refrigerator as soon as possible. Return to room temperature before serving.

To make the herb oil, whizz the herbs and oil in a blender or spice grinder until fairly smooth. Arrange the skewers on a platter and drizzle with the herb oil just before serving.

think ahead   Assemble the skewers up to four hours in advance.

top tip   Buy more tortellini than you need, as some might fall apart in the cooking. Be careful not to overcook – they need to be really al dente. If you can't find buffalo milk mozzarella, use cow's, though not that rubbery pizza variety; settle for cubes of creamy Havarti or Fontina instead.

serve with   These fit best into a buffet with a Mediterranean feel.

deluxe crudités

This sesame dip is the only dip I ever make. I am always asked to divulge the recipe, and people are amazed how something so simple could taste so divine. Even the person who loathes raw vegetables will get some down with this stuff. The dip is best eaten on the day of preparation, as the sesame seeds tend to go soggy.

ingredients

serves 8–10

for the sesame dip:

55g/¼ cup sesame seeds

125g/generous ½ cup Greek (strained plain)
  or thick and creamy yoghurt

125g/generous ½ cup mayonnaise

3 tablespoons dark soy sauce

for the crudités (choose a selection of 4–5):

boiled baby new potatoes

blanched asparagus spears

chicory (Belgian endive) leaves

trimmed radishes, a tiny bit of the top left intact

raw sugar snap peas

celery stalks from the heart, some leaves left on

baby carrots, trimmed

bite-sized broccoli florets

bite-sized cauliflower florets

sliced fennel

method

To make the dip, heat a dry frying pan over a moderate heat. Add the sesame seeds and toast, stirring until they are popping and lightly browned. Transfer to a bowl and leave to cool completely.

Combine the sesame seeds with the yoghurt, mayonnaise and soy sauce and mix very thoroughly. Transfer to a dipping bowl. Arrange the vegetables of your choice on a platter in individual clusters and serve with sesame dip.

hot fennel salt vegan — A good complement to the creamy dip, this tastes particularly good with cherry tomatoes and cucumbers. It's potent stuff — "a dab'll do ya".

ingredients

1 tablespoon rock salt; 8 peppercorns; 1 teaspoon fennel seeds; 1 teaspoon coriander seeds; 1 small dried chilli or ½ teaspoon chilli powder

method

Whizz all the ingredients together in a spice grinder, or use a pestle and mortar to work into a coarse powder. Transfer to a small shallow bowl and serve.

green chargrilled antipasti platter

This blooming platter of succulent vegetables and marinated fresh mozzarella is magnetic – you can make a silly quantity and it's still guaranteed to vanish. You'll need one of those fabulous cast-iron ridged griddle pans (grill pan) for this, ideally a large one that fits over two burners. A smoke-filled kitchen is inevitable (open the windows), but it's the smoke that works the magic on the vegetables. Alternatively, use an outdoor barbecue. Any vegetable responds well to this treatment, but root vegetables should be par-boiled first.

ingredients

serves 8–10

400g/14oz green beans, trimmed

*4 large or 8 small heads of chicory (Belgian endive),
    halved lengthways*

4 fennel bulbs, trimmed and cut into thick slices

2 heads of broccoli, stem peeled, cut into long pieces

*4 tablespoons of olive oil, plus a little extra olive oil,
    for drizzling*

salt and freshly ground black pepper

juice of 1–2 lemons

500g/1lb 2oz mozzarella di bufala, torn into thick shreds

2 garlic cloves

1 teaspoon coarse sea salt

a handful of fresh flat-leaf parsley, chopped

1 bunch of fresh basil, leaves torn

method

Heat a ridged griddle pan (grill pan) over a high heat for 10 minutes, while you get started preparing the vegetables. Place one type of vegetable in a mixing bowl and drizzle lightly with olive oil, then use your hands to coat them all over. Cook one type of vegetable at a time until tender and nicely charred.

Once cooked, return each type of vegetable to the mixing bowl, and season with salt and black pepper. Squeeze lemon juice over the beans, chicory (Belgian endive) and fennel while still hot. Avoid squeezing lemon juice over the broccoli as it may discolour. Leave the vegetables to cool, then store in plastic zip-seal bags in the refrigerator until required.

To prepare the mozzarella marinade, place the torn mozzarella cheese in a large bowl. Pound the garlic with the salt in a mortar. Pound in the parsley until coarsely combined. Whisk in the olive oil and basil. Add the marinade to the mozzarella pieces and stir carefully, then leave to chill in the refrigerator for at least 1 hour. Arrange the charred vegetables on a platter with the marinated mozzarella and serve immediately.

think ahead

This platter can be made up to one day in advance. Store the cooled vegetables in separate zip-seal plastic bags.

top tip

Buffalo mozzarella, made from buffalo's milk, is a luxury and is ideal for this recipe. If unavailable, use fresh cow's milk mozzarella, but not pizza mozzarella. Fresh mozzarella is very vulnerable to spoilage; keep it in the refrigerator until the last moment before combining with the marinade, then refrigerate until ready to serve.

serve with

Leafy salads and plenty of brawny country bread.

a celebration buffet

A beautifully arranged buffet table will inspire lots of "oohs" and "aahs", which is so gratifying. Set it up so that it flows in one direction – left to right is the most logical. Start with a pile of plates at the top end, alongside cutlery wrapped in napkins. Don't squash the food platters up too much – give them room to breathe. Place the dish you anticipate being the most popular at the end of the buffet, which will discourage greed. Don't forget serving spoons, and use medium, not giant, ones.

For a loose leaf salad, instead of making a separate dressing, just dribble some good quality balsamic vinegar and olive oil directly on to the leaves, and toss well with salt and black pepper.

shopping
If there's anything you can get delivered, go for it. Get all shopping out of the way the day before the celebration. If you're cooking over more than one day, try to buy everything in one fell swoop before you get started, but take any perishable items into consideration – look after fresh herbs and vegetables, and pack any dairy or other chilled items in the same bag. Use boxes to pack up your ingredients, it's easier to see what you have than a mess of bags.

crockery
If your budget can possibly stretch to it, consider hiring crockery, and sending it back dirty for an extra small fee.

drinks
If you give people a choice between white wine and champagne, you can guess which one you'll run out of first! If you must limit your supply of bubbly, serve it alone first, then switch to wine. Get champagne flutes as well as wine goblets.

the menu

broccoli & lemon orzo vegan

Orzo is rice-shaped pasta with a toothsome bite. Here's a bright, citrus pasta salad that sings with fresh, green flavour. It's filling yet light, a meal in itself or a delicious accompaniment, making it an ideal buffet or pot-luck dish.

ingredients

serves 8–10

grated zest of 4 lemons

200ml/generous ³/4 cup fresh lemon juice
  (approximately 4 lemons)

4 shallots, finely sliced

salt and freshly ground black pepper

1 teaspoon caster (superfine) sugar

100ml/¹/3 cup olive oil

1 large head of broccoli (approximately 500g/1lb 2oz),
  cut into small florets and stem chopped

100g/3¹/2oz mangetout (snowpeas), trimmed

500g/1lb 2oz orzo

55g/2oz pumpkin seeds

100g/3¹/2oz raw sugar snap peas, sliced

a large handful of fresh flat-leaf parsley, leaves stripped

20 semi-dried tomatoes in oil or 10 sun-dried tomatoes
  in oil, drained and cut into strips

method

Preheat the oven to 200°C/400°F/Gas 6. Bring a large saucepan of water to the boil and salt it well.

Place the lemon zest and juice in a bowl, add the shallots, salt, pepper and sugar, then whisk in the olive oil. Set aside until required. (The shallots should soak in the dressing for a few minutes to become mild and soft.)

Blanch the broccoli and mangetout (snowpeas) in the boiling water for 2 minutes. Remove with a slotted spoon or a sieve, and plunge into a bowl of ice-cold water. Drain when the vegetables are cold.

Add the orzo to the saucepan and cook, stirring frequently, for 6–8 minutes or until cooked (al dente). Drain the orzo and rinse under cold running water until cool. Drain thoroughly and place in a large mixing bowl. Stir through the lemon shallot dressing. Set aside until required.

Place the pumpkin seeds on a baking sheet and toast in the preheated oven for 5 minutes, until golden. Leave to cool.

Add the sugar snap peas, parsley and semi-dried or sun-dried tomatoes to the bowl of orzo and mix thoroughly. Just before serving, stir in the broccoli, mangetout (snowpeas) and toasted pumpkin seeds.

think ahead

This dish can be made up to a day in advance, reserving the broccoli, mangetout (snowpeas) and pumpkin seeds to stir in just before serving.

sugarbeans vegan

Feeding the masses is made a whole lot easier by including these luscious legumes on the menu. It can be made ages in advance, and only gets better as the days go by. Like a really good chutney, it needs time to mature, allowing the rather high quantity of sugar and vinegar to work their magic. It's also very cheap to make in quantity. Water chestnuts are the surprise ingredient in this salad, providing a welcome crunch against all those sweet, creamy beans.

ingredients

serves 10–12
for the salad
500g/1lb 2oz mixed dried beans
200g/7oz French (green) beans or runner (string) beans, cut into
   bite-sized pieces
2 x 225g/8oz cans water chestnuts, drained
1 green (bell) pepper, cut into bite-sized pieces
1 red onion, sliced very finely
for the marinade
125ml/¹/2 cup balsamic vinegar
85g/scant ¹/2 cup caster (superfine) sugar
3 garlic cloves, crushed
2 teaspoon salt
freshly ground black pepper
125ml/¹/2 cup olive oil

method

Soak the dried beans in plenty of cold water overnight, then drain and boil them in fresh water. Let them roll furiously for 10 minutes, then simmer for 50 minutes, until tender, but not falling apart too much. Alternatively, follow the packet instructions. Do taste each type of bean to be sure they are all tender enough. Drain thoroughly.

Bring another small saucepan of water to the boil. Blanch the green beans for 2 minutes, drain and refresh under cold running water or in a bowl of ice-cold water.

Meanwhile, prepare the marinade by whisking together all the ingredients except the olive oil. Beat in the olive oil gradually to emulsify.

Empty the drained cooked beans into a wide, shallow dish and pour over the marinade while they are still hot. Leave to cool, then add the blanched green beans, water chestnuts, green (bell) pepper and red onion. Stir thoroughly. Cover with cling film (plastic wrap) and leave to chill in the refrigerator for at least 24 hours, but preferably longer, stirring now and then. The salad will keep for several days in the refrigerator.

think ahead   This recipe should be started at least 36 hours in advance and can be made up to 4 days in advance.
top tip   This recipe multiplies well, but portions decrease as the number of guests goes up. As part of a buffet containing several cold salads, I have fed 150 on 8 times the recipe. For convenience, buy dried beans already packaged as mixed. The marinade can be made in a blender, but whisk in the oil by hand or else the dressing will appear unappetizingly cloudy.

7-vegetable tagine vegan

Seven is for luck, and this tagine has never failed me. It's a riot of colour and a symphony of flavour. Practically speaking, it's a caterer's dream. Roast the vegetables with whole spices 'til sweet and tender, then stir into a rich sauce. Walk away and leave it overnight to flourish … then all that's left to do is reheat and devour.

ingredients

serves 8–10

300g/10½oz sweet potato, peeled and cut into chunks

300g/10½oz carrots, peeled and cut into chunks

300g/10½oz parsnips or celeriac (celery root), peeled and cut into chunks

1 red and 1 yellow (bell) pepper, cut into chunks

1 large fennel bulb, cut into chunks

1 large red onion, cut into chunks

2 medium courgettes (zucchini), cut into chunks

3 tablespoons olive oil

1 tablespoon cumin seeds

1 tablespoon fennel seeds

salt and freshly ground black pepper

for the sauce:

4 garlic cloves, chopped

3 tablespoons olive oil

400g/14oz can chopped tomatoes

400g/14oz can chickpeas, drained

250ml/generous 1 cup full-bodied red wine

zest and juice of 1 orange

2 cinnamon sticks

12 pitted prunes, halved if large

to serve:

Parsley & Saffron Couscous (see below)

harissa (hot chilli paste; optional)

thick yoghurt (omit for vegans)

method

Preheat the oven to 220°C/425°F/Gas 7. Place all the vegetables in a roasting tin (pan) and coat with the olive oil, whole cumin and fennel seeds, salt and pepper. Roast in the preheated oven for about 30 minutes, until soft and caramelized, stirring once or twice.

Meanwhile to make the sauce, fry the garlic in olive oil. Add the remaining ingredients and simmer until thick. Remove from the heat and combine with the roasted vegetables. If you feel it is too thick, add a little water to achieve the desired consistency. Cover and leave in a cool place overnight. Reheat until piping hot and serve with freshly cooked couscous, harissa and yoghurt.

parsley & saffron couscous vegan — Ideal with the tagine; great on its own.

ingredients

serves 8–10 75g/½ cup large sultanas (golden raisins); 500g/1lb 2oz couscous; 2 teaspoons saffron threads; 1 teaspoon salt; 140g/1 cup whole almonds, toasted; 2 large handfuls of fresh flat-leaf parsley leaves, left whole; grated zest and juice of 3 lemons; 6 tablespoons olive oil; freshly ground black pepper

method

Place the sultanas (golden raisins) in a bowl and soak in boiling water for 15–20 minutes, then drain and set aside. Combine the dry couscous, saffron and salt in a large bowl and stir well. Pour over just enough boiling water to cover. Leave to swell for 5 minutes, then fluff thoroughly with a fork, separating each grain. Place the remaining ingredients in a large bowl and mix thoroughly with soaked sultanas (golden raisins) and couscous. Season as necessary and serve immediately.

giant cheese & spinach pie

Here it is – the ultimate Spanakopita recipe, which my friend Cathy Lowis has passed on from her Greek mother. This classic filo (phyllo) pie is an utterly perfect entertaining recipe – big, bold and easy to multiply, it always succeeds in appealing to everyone, and is usually the favourite dish of the meal. This version has a clever twist with a handful of rice.

ingredients

serves 10–12

for the filling:

2 tablespoons olive oil

6 spring onions (scallions), white and green parts, chopped

750g/1lb 10oz fresh spinach, washed and trimmed, or frozen leaf spinach

350g/1½ cups cottage cheese, drained of any excess whey

500g/2 cups crumbled feta cheese

3 tablespoons chopped fresh dill

3 tablespoons chopped fresh parsley

1 tablespoon uncooked long-grain rice

salt and freshly ground black pepper

for the pastry:

14 large sheets of filo (phyllo) pastry

6 tablespoons olive oil

150g/1½ sticks butter, melted

method

Preheat the oven to 180°C/350°F/Gas 4. To make the filling, heat the oil in a large saucepan over a low to moderate heat. Add the spring onions (scallions) and cook until translucent and soft. Stir in the spinach and cook until just wilted. (If using frozen spinach, cook until heated through.) Drain in a colander and press out as much moisture as possible. Leave to cool, then place on a clean cloth, gather up the sides and squeeze the excess moisture out of the spinach. Chop coarsely.

Combine the spinach with the remaining filling ingredients in a bowl and mix very thoroughly. Taste for seasoning – you may only need to add pepper, as the feta is salty enough.

Unwrap the filo (phyllo) pastry, and if necessary, cut to fit the bottom of a large deep rectangular baking tin (pan) or casserole dish. Cover the pastry with a barely damp cloth to prevent it drying out and becoming brittle. Combine the olive oil and melted butter, then brush the butter mixture all over the baking tin (pan) or casserole dish. Place one layer of filo (phyllo) pastry on the bottom, brush with the melted butter mixture, top with another layer of filo (phyllo) pastry, brush with butter, and so on, forming 7 layers. Spoon all of the filling on top, spreading it out evenly.

Continue layering the filo (phyllo) pastry on top of the filling, again forming 7 layers. Brush the top with the melted butter mixture and then, using a very sharp knife, cut the filo (phyllo) pastry into serving-size diamond shapes (cut vertically down the centre and then diagonally across) or squares.

Bake the pie in the preheated oven for 45 minutes–1 hour, until sizzling, deep golden and crisp right through each of the filo (phyllo) layers. Cut again along the original slits before serving.

think ahead

The filling can be made two days in advance. The whole cooked pie can be frozen, thawed and reheated.

top tip

The filling has a tendency to be on the wet side, but by throwing in a handful of uncooked rice, any excess moisture is absorbed and the bottom stays super-crisp.

serve with

Salad and bread; Sugarbeans (page 38).

roasted asparagus & marbled egg platter

This is a particular favourite around Easter when there is a lot to celebrate, including the start of the asparagus season! The extraordinary method of cooking eggs originates from an ancient Jewish recipe. Making the marbled eggs has become an absolute ritual for me every year, partly because of the fun of it, as well as the romance of the symbolism – fertility and rebirth. I usually slice and caramelize the leftover peeled onions and make soup or a savoury tart.

ingredients

serves 12

12 yellow onions (not red or white)
12 organic eggs
3 tablespoons sunflower oil
4–5 bunches of asparagus spears, trimmed
olive oil, for drizzling
salt and freshly ground black pepper

method

To make the marbled eggs, first peel the onions, reserving every bit of papery skin. Make a layer of onion skins in a saucepan and place the eggs on top, then cover with more onion skins, tucking them in between the eggs. Fill the saucepan with enough water to cover the eggs by at least 2cm/³⁄₄in depth. Add the sunflower oil and bring to the boil, then reduce to a simmer.

After about 30 minutes, lift the eggs out with a slotted spoon and whack gently with another spoon to crack the shells. Return to the onion dye bath and simmer very gently for 5–6 hours, topping up the water as necessary, though the oil will go some way towards preventing evaporation. Leave the eggs to cool in the liquid, then drain and peel, to reveal a beautifully marbled surface. Keep in the refrigerator until ready to serve.

Preheat the oven to 220°C/425°F/Gas 7. To cook the asparagus, place the prepared spears in a roasting tin (pan), drizzle over enough olive oil to just coat the surface and use your hands to coat evenly. Roast the asparagus in the preheated oven for 10–15 minutes, or until done to your taste – ideally until tender but maintaining a little bit of bite. Season to taste with salt and black pepper, then serve warm or cold with the marbled eggs.

think ahead   The eggs can be cooked up to two days in advance and the asparagus up to four hours in advance.
top tip   Snap off the base of the asparagus spears – they will break above the woody end, ensuring tenderness.
serve with   Sesame dip from the Deluxe Crudités, page 31.

3

small courses

brilliant starters, or components of a multi-course feast

The spiritual home of the small course is the entire sun-drenched, olive-rich region of

the Mediterranean. From tapas to meze, little dishes made of exquisite ingredients are designed to get the appetite stimulated on lazy evenings in the sunshine with a chilled glass of wine. Many of these traditional dishes are by default vegetarian – the fertility of the Mediterranean bears such a lush selection of ingredients. Prepared simply, the intention is to enhance the natural beauty of the key ingredient. Throughout the Med, they really know a thing or two when it comes to enjoying life through food.

In modern times, we aim to eat with a light and healthy approach as often as possible. We embrace the food of the Mediterranean for its healthy olive oil and vitamin-rich qualities as much as its sunny flavours. We can also embrace the custom of exciting the appetite and keeping it aroused with every small course, rather than extinguishing it with a big heavy one. This is a rich tradition in Asia as well; at street markets you can enjoy "little eats" – hopping from stall to stall, trying a little bit at each one. It's a far more interesting way to eat, and when you are entertaining, it's an exciting way to cook.

All the recipes in this chapter can be enjoyed as the opening of a fantastic meal, as the components of a feast of little dishes, or simply on their own as a light meal. They can all be served from one platter or bowl, or as individual treats. If you are feeding many, you might wish to plate up individual dishes and have them waiting on the table when the dinner bell rings. Every host should want to spoil the guests, but be judicious with multi-courses, and space them out sensibly – that way every bite will be appreciated.

spiced baby aubergines (eggplants) with minted yoghurt

Indian cooks are fond of stuffing baby aubergines (eggplants), and these are cooked in a South Indian style, filling the house with a rich curry fragrance. Choose teardrop-shaped aubergines (eggplants), about 6cm/2½ in long, and cook them up to 6 hours in advance, combining with the sauce just before serving.

ingredients

serves 4–6

500g/1lb 2oz baby aubergines (eggplants)

300ml/1¼ cups vegetable stock

for the spice oil:

5 tablespoons sunflower oil

2 teaspoons black mustard seeds

4 garlic cloves, finely chopped

2–3 fresh red chillies, finely chopped

1 teaspoon ground turmeric

2 teaspoons cumin seeds

½ teaspoon fenugreek seeds (optional)

½ teaspoon salt

for the sauce:

100ml/generous ⅓ cup thick yoghurt

a handful of fresh mint, chopped

juice of 1 lime

salt and freshly ground black pepper

method

First make the spice oil. Heat the oil in a non-stick frying pan over a moderate to high heat. Add the mustard seeds and when they start to pop, stir in the remaining ingredients. Immediately take the frying pan off the heat and pour the oil into a cold ceramic bowl. Leave the oil to cool. Wipe the cooled frying pan with kitchen paper (paper towels), leaving a light slick of oil.

Meanwhile, prepare the aubergines (eggplants). Grip by the stem end and lay on a chopping board, then, using a very sharp knife, slice the flesh from top to bottom, leaving the stem intact, making 3–4 thin slices. Alternatively, cut them into quarters, again leaving the stem intact.

When the spice oil is cool, use a teaspoon to apply a little oil and spice in between each layer of the sliced or quartered aubergines (eggplants). Secure each one at the bottom with a cocktail stick or wooden skewer. Arrange them in the reheated frying pan and fry over a moderate heat until lightly coloured on one side, then turn over and colour the other side. Pour in the vegetable stock, cover and lower the heat to a simmer. Cook for about 10–15 minutes, until very soft – when prodded with a skewer they should offer no resistance. Remove the lid and raise the heat slightly, and reduce any remaining juices to a thick glaze, which just coats the bottom of the pan.

To make the sauce, combine all the ingredients, then spread the sauce on to a plate, place the aubergines (eggplants) on top and dribble any pan juices over them. Serve warm or cold.

raw thai salad in a poppadom shell vegan

This salad is all crunch and perfume – it really gets the appetite stirring, while being exceptionally light. I created it for a friend's summer wedding. The colourful salads were waiting at each place setting, forming part of the decoration as the guests came into the lavishly floral marquee. It's simple enough to mass produce very successfully, but also works well for a smaller, less formal affair.

ingredients

serves 8–10

for the dressing:

100ml/¹⁄₃ cup golden syrup or corn syrup

2 tablespoons lime juice

¹⁄₄ cup light soy sauce

2 garlic cloves

2–3 small, fresh red chillies, sliced

3 lemon grass sticks, sliced (optional)

4 kaffir lime leaves, stem removed and coarsely chopped (optional)

for the salad:

225g/scant 2 cups shredded red cabbage

1 red (bell) pepper, de-seeded and sliced

350g/2 cups bean sprouts

8 spring onions (scallions), sliced on the diagonal

2 x 200g/7oz cans sliced water chestnuts, drained

4 canned hearts of palm, drained and sliced on the diagonal

4 fresh mint sprigs, leaves stripped

10 leaves from a round lettuce, washed and thoroughly dried

3 tablespoons sesame seeds, toasted (approximately 25g/1oz)

2 limes, cut into wedges

8–10 edible flowers, such as pansies or nasturtiums (optional)

oil, for frying

10 poppadoms

method

To make the dressing, whizz everything in the blender until smooth and set aside until required. Toss the first seven salad ingredients together lightly and keep cool.

Heat a good 10cm/4in depth of oil in a frying pan until it starts to smoke (190°C/375°F). Using tongs, carefully place a poppadom in the oil, then use a ladle to press down in the middle – the poppadom will form a basket around the ladle. Drain upside down on kitchen paper (paper towels). Repeat with other poppadoms and leave to cool.

Line each cooled poppadom with a lettuce leaf. Toss the dressing through the vegetables and spoon into each basket. Sprinkle with the toasted sesame seeds, and finish with a lime wedge and an edible flower (if using).

think ahead

Poppadom shells can be fried four hours in advance and kept in a dry place.

ginger-spiked avocados vegan

If there is a way to improve the heavenly buttery flavour of ripe avocados, then this is it. Ginger and avocado have a surprising affinity. Prepare these as close to serving time as you can.

ingredients

serves 6

3 perfectly ripe avocados

juice of 1–2 lemons

2 tablespoons dark soy sauce

1 tablespoon balsamic vinegar

2 teaspoons finely grated fresh root ginger

freshly ground black pepper

sprigs of dill, to garnish

method

Slice the avocados in half and remove the stone (pit). To extract a complete half from the skin, soak a large spoon in a mug of boiling water for a few seconds, then use it to quickly slide between the skin and the flesh at the narrow end of the avocado. The warmth of the spoon should "melt" the flesh slightly, allowing you to scoop the avocado flesh out in one smooth move. Alternatively, cut the avocados into quarters and peel away the skin. Sprinkle lemon juice over the avocados and use your hands to gently coat them all over. Place on a platter or individual serving plates.

Mix together the soy sauce, vinegar and ginger and drizzle over the avocados or pour into the stone (pit) hole. Finish with a good grinding of black pepper and decorate with sprigs of dill.

roasted spiced pumpkin soup with tamarind vegan

Imagine if velvet could bite, and you get some idea of what this soup tastes like. Buy a dense-fleshed pumpkin or squash weighing about 1.3kg/3lbs for the recipe, to allow for peeling and deseeding.

ingredients

serves 4–6

1kg/2lbs pumpkin flesh, peeled and cut into chunks

1 teaspoon coriander seeds

1 teaspoon cumin seeds

6 garlic cloves

6cm/2¹/2in piece of fresh root ginger, peeled and chopped

salt and freshly ground black pepper

3–4 tablespoons extra virgin olive oil

1litre/4 cups vegetable stock

2 tablespoons tamarind paste (page 17) or

   1 tablespoon brown sauce or 2 teaspoons Worcestershire sauce

to garnish (optional):

double (heavy) cream or plain yoghurt

hulled pumpkin seeds

method

Preheat the oven to 200°C/400°F/Gas 6. Place the pumpkin or squash in a roasting tin (pan) and sprinkle over the spices, whole garlic cloves, ginger, salt and black pepper. Dribble over the olive oil and toss with your hands to coat evenly. Roast in the preheated oven for 30–40 minutes, giving it a stir once or twice, until the pumpkin is very soft.

Leave to cool slightly, then scrape into a saucepan and add the vegetable stock and tamarind paste. Bring to the boil and simmer very gently for 10 minutes. Purée until totally smooth, then serve in warm bowls with a dribble of cream or yoghurt and pumpkin seeds sprinkled over the top.

beetroot (beet) & coconut soup vegan

This soup is an absolute stunner. Coconut and beetroot (beet) are often cooked together in South India, which is the inspiration for this exciting soup. The shocking pink beetroot (beet) is made even brighter on a canvas of milky coconut – and the exotic flavours really do match up to the brilliant appearance. Any soup can be served as a canapé out of tiny espresso cups or shot glasses (allow the soup to cool slightly before pouring into delicate cups or glasses). This one is particularly impressive served in this way.

ingredients

serves 4–6

500g/1lb 2oz fresh beetroot (beet), leaves removed, scrubbed

200g/7oz block of creamed coconut, chopped

1 litre/4 cups vegetable stock

4 garlic cloves, peeled, coarsely chopped or halved

1 teaspoon ground cumin

grated zest of 1 lemon

juice of 1/2 lemon

to serve:

Cucumber Salsa (see below)

pitta breads or chapatis, cut into strips and toasted

method

Bring a large saucepan of water to the boil and salt it well. Add the beetroot (beet) and boil for 30–40 minutes, until tender throughout (test with a skewer or sharp knife). Drain, then rinse under cold running water and rub off the skins, tops and spindly roots. Chop coarsely.

Bring the vegetable stock to the boil in the rinsed-out saucepan, then stir in the coconut until dissolved.

Place the beetroot (beet), garlic, cumin, lemon zest and juice, and about 200ml/generous 3/4 cup water in a blender and purée until smooth.

Add the beetroot (beet) purée to the boiling coconut stock. (You can swirl some coconut stock around the blender to get out every last bit of purée.) Bring to the boil and simmer for 10 minutes. Serve in warm bowls with a spoonful of cucumber salsa on top, and strips of toasted pitta bread or chapati on the side.

cucumber salsa vegan — a clean-tasting salsa that lightens up the soup.

ingredients

5cm/2in piece of cucumber, peeled, de-seeded and very finely chopped; 1 shallot, finely chopped; 10 fresh mint leaves, finely chopped; 1 fresh red chilli, de-seeded and finely chopped; a squeeze of lemon juice; a pinch of salt

method

Simply mix all the ingredients together thoroughly. It benefits from standing for a while, allowing the flavour to develop.

a small feast for friends —

For a laid-back weekend afternoon with friends, escape from the routine starter-main-dessert format – try a casual six-course meal. If you think that sounds like a contradiction in terms, think again. It's an invitation to eat lavishly, but informally. I promise you won't be shopping, chopping and washing up for days.

The idea is simple: six consecutive small dishes, each to be considered and savoured, one after the other. Choose six simple recipes, including something sweet. Some courses could be as simple as boiled artichokes with lemon and mayonnaise, a bowl of twinkling olives or slices of sensuous ripe mango. Don't reveal the menu. It's fun to maintain a sense of excitement and curiosity between courses.

shopping   Seek out a farmer's market or visit an unusual deli in the morning or on the day before. Don't be rigid about your menu. Go with an open mind – you might find a special cheese, some irresistible tomatoes as sweet as cherries, or a bizarre morsel you've never discovered before for everyone to sample.

crockery   You won't need six sets of crockery for this six-course affair. One or two smallish plates and maybe one small bowl per person will suffice. Don't even think about washing dishes until bedtime – or tomorrow.

drinks   Beer seems to encourage laughter more than other drinks. Try buying a selection of different types of beer and ale and sampling a new one with each course. If it's a hot day, serve the beer in chilled glass mugs.

the menu

avocado soup with toasted cheese topping

The avocado is a sensuous and moody creature. When overripe, its incredible buttery texture can almost forgive a slightly off flavour. When underripe, it's totally inedible. Avocados are vulnerable – rough handling destroys them, and so does fierce heat. However, as they have the highest fat content of all fruits, a careful warming brings out the best in them. This recipe, inspired by a soup I ate in Mexico, is essentially a guacamole diluted with hot stock. It's a breeze to make, but just take care not to cook it – merely warm it through.

ingredients

serves 4–6

for the soup:

4 medium ripe avocados

juice of 2 limes

200ml/generous ³/₄ cup crème fraîche or soured cream

1 small onion, finely chopped

2 tomatoes, chopped

1 garlic clove, crushed

1 fresh red chilli, de-seeded and finely chopped

salt and freshly ground black pepper

750ml/3 cups hot vegetable stock

for the topping:

100g/3¹/₂oz corn tortilla chips (unflavoured)

100g/1 cup grated Cheddar or Monterey Jack cheese

4 spring onions (scallions), chopped

100ml/¹/₂ cup crème fraîche or soured cream

method

Preheat the oven or grill (broiler) to its highest setting. Scoop out the avocado flesh and mash it with the lime juice. (A potato masher is the perfect tool for the job.) Stir in the crème fraîche or soured cream, onion, tomato, garlic and chilli, and season to taste with salt and black pepper. Place 4–6 serving bowls on an oven tray and slide them into the oven to warm slightly.

The stock should be hot but not boiling. Stir the stock into the avocado mixture, then ladle into the warmed serving bowls. To make the topping, scatter a few tortilla chips on top of each bowl and sprinkle with the grated cheese. Pop the bowls in the oven or under the grill (broiler) for just a few minutes, until the cheese melts. To serve, top with a few chopped spring onions (scallions) and a dollop of crème fraîche or soured cream and eat immediately.

think ahead

The avocado mixture can be made up to two hours in advance. Cover with cling film (plastic wrap) and keep in the refrigerator, then bring up to room temperature before adding to the stock.

top tip

Presentation is most impressive out of individual bowls, but you can also pour the soup into one large ovenproof dish, allowing plenty of surface area to sprinkle over the tortillas and cheese, then serve from the dish.

serve with

This is quite a filling soup, and can be made into a complete meal with a salad on the side.

warm mushroom salad with creamy caper dressing

Use any mushroom you fancy for this simple yet sophisticated salad. It's easily converted to a main course by adding hard-boiled (hard-cooked) eggs or fried halloumi cheese.

ingredients

serves 4

2 tablespoons butter (approximately 25g/1oz)

1 tablespoon olive oil

2 garlic cloves, sliced

400g/14oz wild mushrooms or field or portobello
  mushrooms, stems removed, thinly sliced

salt and freshly ground black pepper

3 tablespoons finely chopped mixed herbs, such as
  rosemary, sage, thyme, marjoram and parsley

grated zest and juice of 1 lemon

for the dressing:

125ml/½ cup crème fraîche or soured cream

2 tablespoons capers in vinegar, plus 1 teaspoon
  caper vinegar

1 tablespoon chopped fresh chives

1–2 tablespoons water, optional

200g/7oz mixed lettuce leaves

crusty bread, to serve

method

Melt the butter in a large frying pan or preheated wok over a moderate heat, and add the olive oil. Add the garlic and fry until fragrant. Add the mushrooms and season well with salt and black pepper. Stir-fry until the mushrooms are soft, then add the herbs and fry for 5 minutes or so, until most of the pan juices have evaporated. Squeeze the juice of ½ lemon over the mushroom mixture and remove from the heat.

To make the dressing, combine all the ingredients with the remaining lemon juice and zest. If desired, thin slightly with the water. Spoon the warm mushroom mixture over the mixed lettuce leaves and drizzle over the dressing. Serve with bread.

honey-roast parsnip & pear salad with blue cheese dressing

Parsnips, pears and any blue cheese are a harmonious trio. This is an elegant winter salad, which kicks off a meal in style. It's well-balanced nutritionally, with the buttery macadamia nuts for extra protein, so it can also be served as a light main course.

ingredients

serves 4

4 small parsnips, peeled and cut into quarters lengthways

2 tablespoons olive oil

1 tablespoon honey

salt and freshly ground black pepper

2 dessert pears, sliced into wedges

4 handfuls of wild rocket (arugula)

85g/³/4 cup macadamia nuts, toasted

for the dressing:

150g/5¹/2oz Gorgonzola or other strong blue cheese

3 tablespoons white wine vinegar

125ml/¹/2 cup olive oil

method

Preheat the oven to 200°C/400°F/Gas 6. Place the parsnips in a roasting tin (pan) and coat with the olive oil. Drizzle with the honey and season to taste with salt and black pepper. Roast in the preheated oven for about 20 minutes, until golden. Leave to cool.

To make the dressing, mash the Gorgonzola in a bowl. Stir in the vinegar and whisk in the olive oil with a little salt and black pepper, until fairly smooth.

Arrange the rocket (arugula) on individual plates and follow with the pears, toasted nuts and roasted parsnips, then pour over the dressing. Finish with more black pepper.

no-knead honey seed bread

If you love bread with a granular texture, you'll love it even more having made it yourself. To make this sturdy loaf, you will have to get your hands stuck in, but very little elbow grease is required. Seek out hemp seeds – available from health food shops – they have a wonderful nutty crunch, a bit like popcorn.

ingredients

serves 6–8

2 tablespoons honey

1 tablespoon dried (active dry) yeast

300g/2 cups wholemeal (whole-wheat) bread flour

200g/1 ½ cups strong white bread flour

2 teaspoons salt

2 tablespoons hulled pumpkin seeds

2 tablespoons hulled sunflower seeds

2 tablespoons hemp seeds

butter, for greasing

milk, for brushing (optional)

1 tablespoon poppy seeds, for sprinkling (optional)

method

Dissolve the honey in 300ml/1 ¼ cups hand-hot water in a small bowl or jug (pitcher). Whisk in the yeast and leave in a warm place for about 15 minutes, until frothy.

Combine the 2 flours in a mixing bowl. Using a wooden spoon, stir in the salt, pumpkin, sunflower and hemp seeds. Gradually add the yeasty water and mix to a dough. As the dough draws together, put the spoon aside and start using one hand to press the dough into a ball, the other hand to turn the bowl, incorporating everything into a soft, pliable mixture, which leaves the sides of the bowl fairly clean. If the mixture is very sticky, sprinkle in flour bit by bit until a soft dough forms; if it seems too dry, sprinkle in a few drops of water and work it through until the flour disappears.

Grease a baking sheet. Place the dough on it and form into a tapered "eye" shape – or whatever shape you fancy. Dust with flour and cover with a damp tea towel (dishtowel). Leave to rise in a warm place for about 1 hour, until doubled in size. Preheat the oven to 200°C/400°F/Gas 6. Use kitchen scissors to make decorative snips down the middle of the bread. Brush all over with milk and sprinkle with poppy seeds, if desired. Bake the loaf in the preheated oven for 30–40 minutes, until golden, firm and hollow sounding when tapped. Leave to cool on a wire rack.

hot brie fondue — If you're fortunate enough to have access to a serious cheese shop, ask for the *Vacherin du Mont d'Or Sancey Richard*, which is perfect for this treatment. The same method will work with any soft, mature cheese with a washed rind, ideally in a box. If there's no box, you can still wrap the cheese itself in foil – the objective is a hot package of sinfully creamy goo to dip the bread in.

ingredients

serves 6–8; *mature soft cheese in a box; a little white wine*

method

Preheat the oven to 200°C/400°F/Gas 6. Take the lid off the cheese and dribble a bit of white wine over the rind. Replace the lid and wrap the cheese in its box in foil. Place in the preheated oven on the middle rack for 15–20 minutes, after which time the cheese should be liquified right through. Unwrap and dunk slices of the Honey Seed Bread into the warm runny cheese.

4

lunch & dinner

main dishes, some to serve with all the trimmings of a roast dinner

The vegetarian main course seems to be the biggest stumbling block of all for the inexperienced. If you've planned a meal that revolves around a joint of meat, what do you give the veggie? How do you create a "meat substitute"?

The answer is … don't. Soy-based "mock meat" products just don't fit the bill, and the days of the nut roast are now firmly behind us. Most vegetarians will be happy with all the trimmings of a roast dinner like potatoes and vegetables, supplemented with a dish that has loads of flavour and, ideally, a little protein. All of the dishes in this chapter can be slotted into that format. Don't forget, however, that many people will want to share the veggie dish! Make enough to go around the table – it's no fun to be alienated as the vegetarian.

A more interesting way of designing a menu is to give all the elements of the meal equal focus. If meat is being served, let it be one of the elements, but not the main event. Choose four or five dishes which balance each other perfectly. Provide a range of textures, for instance something crisp or crunchy, like lightly cooked green beans with toasted almonds, to contrast with a soft and creamy food like mashed potato. Avoid all the same colour foods, especially brown. Consider the various tastes and aim to balance sweet and sour elements. Always serve one very clean-tasting dish, such as a simple salad or a steamed green vegetable, especially if the rest of the meal is very salty or spicy hot.

Avoid over-complicating matters, however, especially if you're only cooking for a few. All the dishes in this chapter can, of course, be served as meals on their own.

ricotta & herb dumplings with vodka & porcini butter sauce

The Italians would call these dumplings "malfatti", meaning "badly made", because they are irregular in an endearing kind of way, meaning less fuss for the cook. The vodka fleshes out the sauce and turns this into a seriously good dish. It could easily be slotted into a roast dinner – serve from a sizzling casserole on a wooden board, or transfer to a warm serving dish to be passed around with freshly grated Parmesan.

ingredients

serves 4

300g/10¹/₂oz baby spinach, washed

2–6 tablespoons plain (all-purpose) flour

a large handful of fresh herbs, such as basil, parsley or oregano, chopped

500g/1lb 2oz ricotta cheese, drained

3 eggs

60g/2oz fresh Parmesan cheese, grated

2 tablespoons semolina

salt and freshly ground black pepper

for the sauce:

1 tablespoon dried porcini (cèpes) mushrooms (approximately 10g/¹/₄oz)

100g/generous ³/₄ stick butter

2 garlic cloves, chopped

100ml/generous ¹/₃ cup vodka

freshly grated Parmesan cheese, to serve

method

First prepare the porcini (cèpes) for the sauce. Place them in a bowl and pour over enough boiling water to cover. Leave to soak for 15 minutes, then drain, rinse again and chop. For the dumplings, bring a large saucepan of salted water to the boil, then reduce to a simmer.

Meanwhile, place the spinach in a colander and pour boiling water directly over until it is wilted, then drain well, pressing out as much moisture as you can. Squeeze in a clean cloth to dry out further. Place the spinach in a food processor with the remaining ingredients – start with 2 tablespoons flour and pulse until well mixed. Alternatively, chop the spinach and herbs, then beat with the other ingredients in a bowl. The mixture should have the consistency of cottage cheese – it should just drop off the spoon.

The water in the saucepan should be simmering gently. Drop one test spoonful of the mixture into the water – don't panic if it falls apart, just add more flour to the mixture, then drop in spoonfuls and boil until they rise to the top, about 2–3 minutes. Drain thoroughly in a kitchen paper (paper towel) lined colander. Cook in batches and keep warm in a dish in the oven.

To make the sauce, melt the butter in a frying pan. Add the garlic and prepared porcini (cèpes) and fry for 2 minutes. Add the vodka and season to taste with salt and pepper. Return to the boil, then simmer for 2 minutes, until the alcohol fumes are gone. Spoon over the dumplings, and be generous with the Parmesan.

grilled tofu & mango skewers vegan

Anyone who doesn't like tofu should consider this: it just needs a little TLC to transform it from boring to irresistible. Frying gives it a yummy crisp texture, and marinating kicks its sponge-like talents into action, as it drinks up a pungent sauce.

ingredients

serves 4–5

for the sauce

4 tablespoons dark soy sauce

2 tablespoons golden (corn) syrup or honey

1 tablespoon chilli sauce, or 5–6 shakes Tabasco sauce

2 tablespoons lime juice

1 tablespoon finely grated root ginger

for the skewers

300g/10½oz firm tofu, drained and patted dry

4 tablespoons cornflour (cornstarch)

vegetable oil, for frying

1 small ripe but firm mango, cubed

10 kaffir lime leaves (optional)

10 lime wedges

method

Pour boiling water over 10 long wooden skewers and leave to cool; this should prevent them from burning on the grill (broiler). Mix together the sauce ingredients and set aside.

Sprinkle the cornflour (cornstarch) over a plate. Cut the tofu into 20 x 1cm/½in chunks and roll in the cornflour (cornstarch), shaking off any excess. Heat about 1cm/½in depth of oil in a wide frying pan until hot but not smoking. Fry the tofu, turning once with tongs, until crisp and golden all over. Keep the pieces from touching or they may stick together. Drain on kitchen paper (paper towels) briefly, then transfer to a plate. Spoon half the sauce over the hot tofu and leave to cool. If you have time, it will improve further if left to marinate for 1–2 hours in the refrigerator.

Thread a piece of mango, a piece of tofu, a lime leaf (if using), another piece of tofu, mango and finishing with a lime wedge on to each skewer. Heat a ridged griddle pan (grill pan) over a high heat, or heat the oven grill (broiler) to high. Grill the skewers, using tongs to turn them, until lightly charred all over. If the pan is hot, the cooking process should be quick, as the tofu is already fried. Use any remaining sauce to flavour accompanying noodles or rice.

smoked aubergine (eggplant) relish vegan — A sensational complement to the skewers.

ingredients

1 long, thin aubergine (eggplant); ¼ cucumber, de-seeded and diced; a handful of fresh chives, snipped; 1 fresh green chilli, de-seeded and chopped; 2 tablespoons chopped fresh mint; 1 tablespoon fresh lime juice; 1 tablespoon light soy sauce; 1 teaspoon caster (superfine) sugar

method

Push a fork into the stem of the aubergine (eggplant) and carefully place the body directly on to a high gas flame. Turn occasionally until completely soft and collapsed; the skin should be blackened to the point of ash in places, and steam should be escaping through the fork holes. Alternatively, prick with a fork and grill (broil) until blistered all over.

Transfer to a plate and leave to cool, then peel off the charred skin and chop up the flesh. Don't worry if a few little charred bits remain as they will add to the flavour. Combine the flesh with the remaining ingredients and serve.

sweet potato gnocchi with dolcelatte sauce

Gnocchi, classic Italian potato dumplings, can be a tad stodgy, so here's a little twist on them. Orange-fleshed sweet potato lightens them up beautifully. This minimalist cheese sauce is rather sinful, but goes outrageously well with sweet potato. When choosing sweet potato, rub a tiny speck of the skin off to be sure the flesh is orange. This is a rich dish and a little goes a long way – small portions are best; it's also very appetizing as a first course.

ingredients

serves 4–6
for the gnocchi:
500g/1lb 2oz orange-fleshed sweet potato, scrubbed
salt and freshly ground black pepper
2 egg yolks
75g/generous 1/2 cup plain (all-purpose) flour

52g/1/3 cup semolina, plus extra for dusting
for the sauce:
150ml/2/3 cup single (light) cream
200g/7oz dolcelatte or Gorgonzola cheese, cubed

method

Preheat the oven to 220°C/425°F/Gas 7. Prick the sweet potatoes and roast in the preheated oven for 45 minutes– 1 hour, until soft. Leave until cool enough to handle, then peel.

Mash the flesh with a potato masher and fold in the remaining ingredients. Using wet hands, roll the dough into little dumplings and place on a large baking sheet dusted with semolina. Bring a large saucepan of salted water to the boil, drop the dumplings into the boiling water and boil until they rise to the surface, about 3–4 minutes, then drain.

To make the sauce, heat the cream gently to boiling and stir in the cheese until it melts. Grind in some black pepper and serve immediately, poured over the gnocchi.

roasted aubergines (eggplants) & halloumi with almond sauce

Based on a fifteenth-century Italian recipe, this exotic-tasting sauce uses pomegranate molasses, an amazing sweet and sour syrup made from pure concentrated juice. It is also delicious drizzled over soft white salty cheese.

ingredients

serves 4

2 medium aubergines (eggplants)

olive oil, for brushing

salt and freshly ground black pepper

250g/9oz halloumi cheese, thinly sliced
   (vegans: use tempeh)

300g/10½oz baby spinach, washed

a handful of fresh mint leaves, torn

for the sauce:

4 tablespoons ground almonds

1 tablespoon pomegranate molasses
   (or 1 tablespoon balsamic vinegar) blended with
   4 tablespoons water

1 teaspoon caster (superfine) sugar

1 teaspoon cinnamon

1 teaspoon grated fresh root ginger

1 small garlic clove, crushed

method

Preheat the oven to 220°C/425°F/Gas 7. Cut the stem end off the aubergines (eggplants) and discard, then cut into 4 long wedges. Score the flesh in one diagonal direction, without piercing the skin. Brush thoroughly with olive oil and season to taste with salt and black pepper. Roast for 15–20 minutes, until soft and golden. Keep warm.

Now cook the cheese in a dry frying pan until golden on both sides. To make the sauce, pound everything together in a mortar until smooth. If left to stand, the sauce will thicken; dilute with more water if necessary – it should have the consistency of creamy houmous. Arrange the spinach on a serving plate, then top with the cooked aubergine (egg plant) and cheese. Spoon the sauce over them, or on the side. Sprinkle the torn mint on top and serve.

truffle-scented stuffed mushrooms

Wild about mushrooms? Well, here's a real funghi-fest. There's something so seductive about the deep dark hue, rich flavour, and a texture which can only be described as, well, meaty.

ingredients

serves 6, or 3 generous servings of 2 mushrooms each

6 medium field, flat or portobello mushrooms, similar in size, plus an extra 150g/5½ oz

olive oil

6 teaspoons truffle oil, plus an extra 1½ tablespoons

salt and freshly ground black pepper

250g/9oz shiitake mushrooms, stems removed

5 garlic cloves, sliced

125ml/½ cup Madeira wine, sherry or vermouth

2 teaspoons fresh thyme leaves

a good grinding of nutmeg

55g/2oz fresh Parmesan cheese, grated

a generous handful of fresh flat-leaf parsley leaves

method

Preheat the oven to 200°C/400°F/Gas 6. Cut the stems out of the 6 stuffing mushrooms, then brush the caps generously with olive oil and lay gill-side up on a baking sheet. Drizzle 1 teaspoon truffle oil over the gills of each mushroom and season to taste with salt and black pepper. Coarsely chop the remaining mushrooms, including the shiitakes.

To make the filling, heat 2 tablespoons of olive oil in a frying pan. Add the garlic and fry for a couple of minutes until fragrant. Add the chopped field and shiitake mushrooms, salt and a generous grinding of black pepper. Fry over a medium–high heat, until the mushrooms have collapsed. Pour in the Madeira wine, add the thyme and nutmeg, raise the heat and cook until the juices have mostly evaporated. Leave to cool briefly, then place in a food processor with the grated Parmesan, parsley and the remaining truffle oil. Process until a purée results, then spoon the mixture into the mushroom hollows and bake in the preheated oven for 20–30 minutes, until shrunken and lightly golden on top.

think ahead	The filling can be made twenty-four hours in advance.
top tip	If you are fortunate enough to have a fresh truffle, by all means use it – 1 tablespoon of shavings in the filling mixture would be enough, plus a little more shaved over the finished article. In lieu of truffle oil you could also use 1–2 tablespoons of truffle paste, sold as "salsa truffina". I don't recommend truffles in brine.
serve with	Delicious with polenta, especially grilled (broiled), for added bite; or bruschetta, to accommodate the juices. These go beautifully with roast dinner trimmings.

a fancy Sunday dinner —

The Sunday roast is a bit of a dinosaur, but it's not extinct yet. It's a valuable ritual of family security, when loved ones gather to share gossip, relive old tales and revel in unlimited comfort food. All too often these days, it's reserved for holidays like Thanksgiving and Christmas, but it could be welcomed any weekend. These occasions should be spoiling, but never strenuous; dinner's ready when it's ready. Relax, and have fun introducing a little adventure into the traditional menu.

Roast potatoes are an absolute must-have for this sort of menu, and here's the winning formula: peel potatoes and par-boil for 5–10 minutes, until slightly floury on the outside but hard in the middle, then drain. Shake them around in a roasting pan to rough them up, coat with plenty of olive oil, season and roast in a 220°C/425°F/Gas 7 oven for 40–50 minutes until golden brown and crispy.

shopping   This is an indisputably wintery menu, characterized by the seasonal, rib-clinging ingredients and substantial cooking time. Shopping might involve a bracing whip around the outdoor market; prepare to bundle up and join the hustle and bustle. If you've got several guests coming, make your life easier and delegate shopping or even whole cooked dishes.

crockery   If you've got a fine set, now's the time to get it out. Polish the silver, shine up the glasses that go "ping!", light the candles, relish the ritual.

drinks   A top-notch, full-bodied red wine is the ideal choice. A mid-priced Shiraz or Rioja seems to go miles further than plonk, as every sip is savoured.

the menu

gratin of roasted garlic & squash *80*

ricotta & herb dumplings with vodka & porcini butter sauce *67*

roast potatoes *74*

steamed tender-stem broccoli

radicchio & tomato salad drizzled with balsamic vinegar

cranberry torte with hot toffee-brandy sauce *90*

simple asparagus tarts

I affectionately call these "asparagus in a frame". I first devised this recipe for a large party on a minuscule budget, to be inexpensive (it was asparagus season) as well as low labour. Afterwards, I got calls from many of the guests, asking me to make them one or two, which I gladly agreed to, since they only take ten minutes to make.

ingredients

serves 4–8
500g/1lb 2oz medium thickness asparagus spears, trimmed
2 teaspoons semolina or polenta
375g/13oz ready-rolled puff pastry
2 egg yolks

100ml/^{1}/$_2$ cup crème fraîche or soured cream
a pinch of salt
freshly ground black pepper
60g/generous ^{1}/$_2$ cup freshly grated Parmesan cheese

method

Preheat the oven to 220°C/425°F/Gas 7. Bring a saucepan of salted water to the boil. Add the asparagus, return to the boil and cook for 3 minutes. Drain under cold running water until cool, then pat dry.

Sprinkle the semolina or polenta over a large baking sheet, or over 2 small ones. Divide the pastry into 2 rectangles and place on the sheet. Using a sharp knife, score a 1.5cm/^{3}/$_4$in border around the edge of the pastry, not cutting through completely. Arrange the asparagus inside the "pastry frames". To ensure that each slice has a fair share of the delicious tips, alternate the direction of the tips. Mix together the egg yolks, crème fraîche or soured cream and seasoning in a measuring jug. Pour the mixture evenly into the middle of the 2 pastry frames, which should allow the borders to puff up in the oven before the custard runs off the edge. Quickly sprinkle the Parmesan over the 2 pastries and place in the preheated oven immediately.

Bake for 20–30 minutes, until the pastry is deep golden and the custard is patched with gold. Serve warm, each tart cut into 4 pieces. Cold tarts can be successfully reheated in an oven at 200°C/400°F/Gas 6 for 5–7 minutes.

potato, garlic & smoked mozzarella strudel

Strudel literally means "whirlwind", but this one is a breeze to make. Ready-made puff pastry is an honourable convenience, and when ready-rolled is easy to use. All-butter pastry has the best flavour and flakiest texture.

ingredients

serves 6–8

750g/1lb 10oz floury (mealy) potatoes, peeled and
    cut into chunks
3 small garlic cloves
1 teaspoon coarse sea salt

250g/9oz smoked mozzarella, or other smoked cheese,
    cut into 1cm/½in cubes
3–4 tablespoons finely chopped fresh flat-leaf parsley
freshly ground black pepper
375g/13oz ready-rolled puff pastry
1 egg yolk mixed with 1 tablespoon milk, for glazing

method

Bring a saucepan of water to the boil and salt it well. Add the potatoes and simmer for about 15 minutes, until the potatoes are soft. Drain and mash, then leave to cool. Using a mortar and pestle, pound the garlic with the coarse salt until a smooth purée results. Add the purée to the cooled potatoes, along with the smoked mozzarella and parsley. Grind a good dose of black pepper into the mixture and stir until thoroughly combined.

Lay the pastry out on a baking sheet. Spoon the potato mixture into a long, well-compacted sausage-shape on one side of the pastry edge, leaving a border on that side, and plenty of pastry to fold over the top of the mixture on the other side. Smooth the mixture and fold the pastry all the way around forming a stuffed tube. Seal the ends by pressing the pastry together. Press together the long seam, then roll the strudel over to rest with the seam underneath.

Cover and leave to chill in the refrigerator for 30 minutes, or up to 48 hours. When ready to bake, preheat the oven to 220°C/425°F/Gas 7. Using a sharp knife, make diagonal slashes on the top of the strudel about 2cm/¾in apart and brush all over with egg–milk mixture. Bake in the oven for 30–40 minutes, until deep golden and crispy all over. Leave to cool for at least 5 minutes, then slice into portions along the slashes.

sweet onion & ricotta cheesecake with cranberries & sage

This is my holiday version of Viana La Place's "Tortino di Cipolla" from *Verdura*, her brilliant book of Italian vegetable recipes. I have gussied it up with cranberries – a little vulgar maybe, but very Christmassy, and a nice tart contrast to the sweet onions. When cranberries are out of season, make it without.

ingredients

1kg/2lb 4oz fresh ricotta cheese

3 tablespoons olive oil, plus extra for greasing and drizzling

350g/12oz onions (approximately 2 large), chopped

4 garlic cloves, chopped

10 fresh sage leaves, coarsely chopped

4 eggs, beaten

6 tablespoons freshly grated Parmesan cheese

salt and freshly ground black pepper

150g/1 cup fresh or frozen cranberries

55g/2oz cracker crumbs (cream crackers or saltines),
  finely crushed

whole fresh sage leaves, to garnish (optional)

method

Preheat the oven to 190°C/375°F/Gas 5. Place the ricotta in a sieve and stand over a bowl or the sink. Leave to drain thoroughly while you cook the onions.

Heat the olive oil in a large frying pan over a low heat. Add the onions and cook gently, stirring frequently, until very soft, but not coloured. Add the garlic and sage and cook for 1–2 minutes, until fragrant.

Beat together the drained ricotta, eggs, Parmesan, salt and pepper (ideally in a food processor) until totally smooth. Stir in the onion mixture and cranberries and mix thoroughly.

Brush a 22cm/8½in springform tin (pan) generously with olive oil. Sprinkle the cracker crumbs evenly over the bottom and sides, then pour in the ricotta mixture and smooth the surface with a spatula. Garnish the top with whole sage leaves and drizzle a little olive oil over the top, especially over the sage leaves. Place on a baking sheet and bake in the preheated oven for 45 minutes–1 hour, until firm and golden. Leave to cool for about 10 minutes, then transfer to a serving plate. Serve warm or cold.

think ahead

This recipe can be made up to twenty-four hours in advance. Leave to cool, then cover and keep in the refrigerator. If serving warm, return to room temperature before reheating.

top tip

Try to get ricotta from an Italian deli or high-quality cheese shop, as it will probably be less watery and more suitable for cooking than the supermarket tubs.

serve with

Roast dinner trimmings.

gratin of roasted garlic & squash

This is serious comfort food – a pretty outrageous dish that always pleases everyone. The squash family is huge and some members are more agreeable than others. Choose one with a dark orange, creamy, dense flesh. Butternut, kaboucha, acorn and onion squash are all good bets.

ingredients

serves 4–6

3 tablespoons extra virgin olive oil

2 butternut squashes or other sweet-fleshed pumpkins
    or squashes (approximately 2kg/4^1/2lb)

8 garlic cloves

8 fresh sage leaves

250g/9oz Gruyère cheese, cut into 1cm/^{1}/2in cubes

salt and freshly ground black pepper

method

Preheat the oven to 220°C/425°F/Gas 7. Chop the stem off the squash, then use a vegetable peeler or paring knife to peel off the skin. (This is much easier to do at this stage than after cooking.) Slice the squash in half from stem to base, then scoop the seeds out with a spoon and lay the squash on a baking sheet, cavity side up. Place 2 whole cloves of garlic in each cavity, along with 2 sage leaves. Pour about 2 teaspoons of olive oil over the garlic and sage and, using a pastry brush, paint the oil all over the surface of the flesh. Bake in the preheated oven for 30–40 minutes, until tender and lightly browned around the edges. Leave to cool slightly.

Place the flesh in a bowl along with the roasted garlic and sage. Mash it all together with a potato masher until crushed, but not entirely smooth. Stir in the Gruyère cubes. Spoon into a presentable, greased gratin dish and bake in the oven for 15–20 minutes, until golden and bubbly. Serve right away.

think ahead

Roast the squash one day in advance.

top tip

If you can't find a good squash, use red sweet potato. Roast whole in the skin at the same temperature, adding the garlic and sage for the last twenty minutes, lightly oiled alongside, then leave to cool and peel before mashing.

serve with

Roast dinner accompaniments; salad; steamed green vegetables.

5

desserts

little sweeties and naughty bits

As if you haven't spoiled your guests enough already, you can really go to town with dessert. It's your gratifying grand finale, and no time to be judicious – everyone should feel they can dive into a dessert with reckless abandon, even if they thought they couldn't manage another bite. Dessert brings out the greedy child in all of us.

At canapé parties, some little sweet bites towards the end of the evening are a great way to inject some sugary stimulation, but can also be a signal that the party may be nearing an end. Make Baby Lemon Curd Meringues (page 96), or make the Pecan Chocolate Ripple Cheesecake (page 98) in a large square baking dish and cut into bite-sized portions.

If you're feeding a big crowd, choose Rhubarb Soup with Ginger-studded Meringues (page 88) or one type of Eton Mess (page 87). If you're really pushed, they won't know what they're missing if you buy one, giant, delicious, ripe cheese – or two or three; any more and it's overkill – and some delectable crackers. Avoid buying lots of little pieces of different cheeses; the cheeseboard will quickly look unappetizing, and people will feel they can only take a small portion. Encourage your guests to surrender to temptation.

marrons caramelises au cognac

Chestnuts in a Cognac sauce (sorry, but it just sounds so much better in French) — a quick and easy way to turn plain old ice cream into something unforgivably wicked. It's a great emergency dessert.

ingredients	serves 4–6
	250g/9oz whole peeled cooked chestnuts (sold in a vacuum pack, or in cans)
	4 tablespoons salty butter (approximately 55g/2oz)
	3 tablespoons sugar
	100ml/1/3 cup Cognac or brandy
	chocolate ice cream, to serve
method	Carefully separate the chestnuts. Melt the butter in a frying pan over a moderate heat. Add the chestnuts and sauté gently for 2 minutes. Sprinkle in the sugar, stir and boil until it dissolves, about 1 minute. Pour in the Cognac, stir and turn off the heat. Leave to stand until just warm, then spoon over the ice cream.
think ahead	This is a last minute recipe, but chestnuts and Cognac are kitchen cupboard must-haves.
top tip	Make this as soon as the meal is finished. In the time it takes to cool off and thicken a little, your appetite should have had just enough time to come back for more. (If you have a very efficient freezer, you may want to get the ice cream out to soften as well).
serve with	Vanilla ice cream is also lovely with this.

tropical eton mess

Eton Mess is the absolute best dessert to feed a large, discerning crowd, as I'm sure the dinner ladies at the posh boys' school know all too well — traditionally it's been served at Eton College's Founders' Day and Fourth of June celebrations. The classic version is a demure strawberry affair. Here are my two show-stoppers.

ingredients

serves 8

8 individual hard-cooked meringue nests

600ml/2½ cups double (heavy) cream

4 tablespoons white rum (optional)

1 papaya, peeled, de-seeded and chopped

1 small mango, peeled and chopped

1 baby pineapple, peeled and chopped, or 500g/1lb 2oz fresh prepared pineapple

2 ripe passion fruit

physalis, to decorate

method

Break up the meringues into bite-sized pieces in a large bowl. Whip the cream until it holds its shape — do not over beat — then stir in the rum.

Just before serving, fold the crushed meringues and whipped cream together until evenly mixed. Spoon into a serving bowl and top with the prepared fruit. Slice open the passion fruits and dribble the juice and seeds over the top. Decorate, if desired, with physalis.

strawberry rose eton mess — Follow the recipe above, replacing the fruit with about 500g/1lb 2oz
fresh hulled strawberries, halved if large. Instead of the rum, beat 4 tablespoons rosewater through the cream. Provide extra strawberries in a bowl on the side.

rhubarb soup with ginger-studded meringues

This one is excellent for a crowd as the portions are quite flexible, and people can easily serve themselves. It looks beautiful served from a big, wide, shallow bowl, with the marshmallow-centred meringues floating on top.

ingredients

serves 10–12

2kg/4lb 8oz rhubarb, trimmed and sliced into
  1cm/½in pieces
250g/1½ cups caster (superfine) sugar
crème fraîche or thick and creamy yoghurt, to serve

for the meringues:

3 egg whites
175g/generous ¾ cup caster (superfine) sugar
1 teaspoon cornflour (cornstarch)
½ teaspoon vinegar
55g/⅓ cup crystallized ginger, chopped

method

Place the rhubarb in a saucepan with the sugar and 400ml/1¾ cups water. Cover, bring to the boil and simmer for 20–30 minutes, until a medium-thin compote results. Pour into a bowl, leave to cool, then chill thoroughly.

To make the meringues, preheat the oven to 120°C/250°F/Gas ½, and line a large baking sheet with baking paper (parchment paper). Beat the egg whites until stiff, then beat in the sugar, 1 tablespoon at a time, until the mixture is very stiff and glossy. Whisk in the cornflour (cornstarch), vinegar and ginger pieces. Spoon egg-sized mounds on to the baking sheet, allowing a little space between them for expansion. Bake in the oven for 30 minutes, until crisp on the outside, but still gooey in the middle. When cooled, dislodge the meringues from the paper by sliding a large knife under them.

To serve, pour the soup into a wide, shallow bowl and float the meringues on top. Serve with crème fraîche or yoghurt.

kaffir lime ice cream

The splendid perfume of kaffir lime leaves gives this ice cream a subtle, fragrant undertone. I implore you, make the ice cream without kaffir lime leaves if you can't find them, as this is fantastically easy and delicious, made just with lime juice or even lemon juice. You don't need an ice cream maker, just a freezer.

ingredients

serves 10–12
600ml/2½ cups double (heavy) cream
600ml/2½ cups full cream (whole) milk
350g/2 cups caster (superfine) sugar

6 kaffir lime leaves
150ml/⅔ cup fresh lime juice
zest of 2 limes

method

Mix together the cream, milk and 225g/8oz/1 cup sugar in a large plastic container and stir until the sugar dissolves. Cover tightly and place in the freezer.

Tear the lime leaves away from their tough stems, then pound them in a pestle and mortar to release the fragrant oils. Alternatively, whack them with a rolling pin or similar. Mix together the lime juice, zest, kaffir lime leaves and remaining sugar in a small plastic container and stir until the sugar dissolves (If you prefer, you can whizz the lime leaf mixture in a blender until smooth.) Cover and place in the freezer.

Freeze both containers for about 3 hours, until slushy – the creamy mixture should be the consistency of a milkshake. Scrape the lime mixture into the cream mixture, stirring well and scraping crystals away from the edge of the container. Freeze until solid. The ice cream does freeze very hard, so it's a good idea to thaw it ever so slightly in the refrigerator about 1 hour before serving.

cranberry torte with hot toffee-brandy sauce

This incredibly luscious cake is the perfect, lighter alternative to that heavy Christmas pudding or laborious pumpkin pie. It's a cake tin full of sharp fruit and nuts just fused together with a little cardamom-spiked cake batter, then drenched in hot boozy toffee.

ingredients

serves 8–10

500g/1lb 2oz cranberries (fresh or frozen)
85g/³/4 stick butter, melted, plus extra for greasing
200g/1 cup caster (superfine) sugar, divided ¹/2 and ¹/2
150g/1 cup chopped pecans
1 egg, beaten
60g/¹/2 cup sifted plain (all-purpose) flour
1 teaspoon cardamom seeds, crushed in a mortar
3 tablespoons golden granulated sugar
for the sauce
180g/scant 1 cup dark brown sugar
115g/1 stick butter
125ml/¹/2 cup double (heavy) cream
3 tablespoons brandy

method

Preheat the oven to 180°C/350°F/Gas 4. Wash the cranberries and drain well. Grease and line the base of a 24cm/9¹/2in springform cake tin (pan) with baking paper (parchment paper). Place the cranberries in the tin (pan), then sprinkle with half the caster (superfine) sugar and pecans and mix well.

Next, make the batter. Beat the remaining caster (superfine) sugar with the egg in a bowl until well blended. Add the flour, melted butter and cardamom, mix well and pour evenly over the cranberries. Sprinkle the granulated sugar evenly over the top and bake in the preheated oven for 40–45 minutes or until set. Leave to cool in the tin (pan).

To make the sauce, place the sugar, butter and cream in a saucepan. Stir together over a gentle heat until the sugar is dissolved and the sauce is bubbling. Remove from the heat and stir in the brandy.

Use a sharp knife or cake slicer to gently unmould the torte, leaving it on the tin base. Slice into wedges and serve warm or cold, with warm toffee-brandy sauce.

think ahead

The torte can be made 8 hours in advance. The sauce can be made up to 48 hours in advance; cover, keep in the refrigerator and reheat before serving.

top tip

Cranberries have a short season, but they freeze incredibly well – so stock up while they're available and use straight from the freezer in this recipe, any time of year.

a garden tea party —

A relaxing and indulgent tea party is a comfort zone where kids, adults and the elderly are most at ease together. It can also be a useful context for gathering people who don't know each other too well. It's a refreshing way to make the most of sunny days: nibbling, gossiping, celebrating for the sake of it.

The menu here is for a real humdinger of a tea party, a truly lavish affair. For a simpler version, the Cucumber & Herbed Mascarpone Bites (page 15) are essential, then choose one of the three sweet recipes. Supplement with scones (easy to bake, easier to buy) and crumpets or madeleines from a reputable bakery. Don't forget the butter, cream and jam!

shopping · Decorate your table. Buy flowers, lots of fruit and plenty of milk and sugar cubes for tea.

crockery If you're short on tea service, ask a friend or two to bring what cups and saucers they have, then create a funky new set by mixing cups with non-matching saucers. Extra teapots will be a godsend.

drinks Not everyone likes black tea (such as English Breakfast); provide some herbal alternatives. Green tea is delicious, but remember, it's not caffeine-free. To make the perfect pot of tea: warm the teapot with a little boiling water and swirl; discard the water; add teabags or loose tea; then add water, which is on a rolling boil. Brew it fairly strong, and provide a teapot of plain hot water for those who like it weak.

the menu

grilled (broiled) stuffed peaches

Good peaches can be hard to come by. Sometimes they look perfect, but have been picked unripe and taste sour and woolly. If you can, buy one from the batch and take a bite: it should be bursting with sweet juice. White peaches are often the best bet.

ingredients

serves 6

3 ripe peaches, halved and stoned (pitted)
1 tablespoon sugar
high-quality vanilla ice cream, to serve

for the stuffing:

2 tablespoons butter, softened (approximately 25g/1oz)
25g/¼ cup shelled pistachio nuts, finely chopped
2 tablespoons sugar
3 tablespoons brandy
a pinch of ground cloves
1 tablespoon chopped crystallized ginger

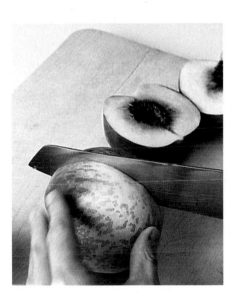 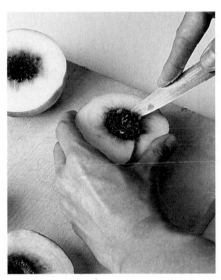 

method

Preheat the grill (broiler) to its highest setting. Beat together the stuffing ingredients until smooth. Place the peach halves in an ovenproof dish. Divide the stuffing evenly between the peaches and sprinkle with the remaining sugar. Cook under the grill (broiler) for about 7–8 minutes, until the stuffing is golden and the sugar is melted. Serve with small scoops of vanilla ice cream.

think ahead

This recipe can be made and assembled up to four hours in advance. Cover and leave to chill in the refrigerator, then allow to return to room temperature before grilling (broiling).

top tip

Vegans should use margarine instead of butter. Avoid "clingstone" peaches – you really need to get that stone (pit) out neatly. Do not store peaches in the refrigerator, or their texture may deteriorate. Ready-shelled pistachios are not the easiest ingredient to find, but you don't need masses of them, so you could shell them yourself. Hulled pumpkin seeds can be substituted.

serve with

Ice cream is ideal, though creamy yoghurt or crème fraîche will do.

baby lemon curd meringues

Make these just bite-sized, as a sweet canapé, or slightly larger, as a light dessert. The meringues can be made up to two days in advance and kept in an airtight container in the refrigerator.

ingredients

serves 8
butter, for greasing
250–300ml/1–1¼ cups crème fraîche,
* soured cream or softly whipped cream*
150–200ml/²/3–³/4 cup top quality lemon curd
pomegranate seeds, redcurrants or blueberries,
* or a mixture*
icing (confectioners') sugar, for dusting

for the meringues:
6 egg whites, at room temperature
a pinch of salt
375g/2 cups caster (superfine) sugar
2 teaspoons cornflour (cornstarch)
1 teaspoon vinegar

method

To make the meringue mixture follow the recipe on page 88, adding the salt with the sugar and omitting the ginger. Place egg-sized fluffy mounds on a lined baking sheet leaving a little room in between each. (You may wish to make them even smaller, for canapés.) Flatten the top of the meringues very slightly and remember, irregularity is beautiful.

Bake the meringues in the preheated oven for 30–40 minutes, until crisp and light golden on the outside, but still a little gooey in the middle. Leave to cool completely on the sheet. Loosen the cold meringues with a palette knife (spatula) and place on a tray. Top each with a spoonful of crème fraîche, whipped cream or soured cream, and a small spoonful of lemon curd; finish with pomegranate seeds, redcurrants or blueberries. Dust with icing (confectioners') sugar, if desired, and serve immediately.

chocolate strawberry truffle pots

These exquisite, rich little pots are ideal after a satisfying meal, when all you want is a few mouthfuls of naughty sweet-ness, without the bulk. Make them up to 8 hours in advance.

ingredients

serves 10
1 large apple, for holding strawberries
200g/7oz high-quality white chocolate
10 equal-sized strawberries.

10 silver sugar pearls (dragées)
250g/9oz luxury plain (semisweet) chocolate
4 tablespoons butter, cubed
300ml/1 1/4 cups double (heavy) cream

method

Slice the stem off the strawberries so they have a flat surface on which to stand upright. Select a large plate and clear a space in the fridge to accommodate it. Melt the white chocolate in a bowl set over simmering water. Dip the pointed end of a strawberry into the melted chocolate to come half way up the berry, then rest cut side down on the plate. Press a sugar pearl (dragée) into the chocolate at the very tip, if desired. Repeat with all the strawberries, then chill.

Arrange 10 shot glasses or bowls on a tray, ready to be filled. Place the plain (semisweet) chocolate, butter and cream in a saucepan, and place over a very gentle heat. Stir constantly until absolutely smooth, then remove from the heat. (If the mixture curdles from overheating, add more cream.) Divide the truffle mixture between the shot glasses or bowls, then place a chilled strawberry, white-chocolate-side-up, on top of the truffle mixture. Leave to chill for about 30 minutes, until set. Allow to return to room temperature before serving.

pecan chocolate ripple cheesecake

I created this for my mother's 70th birthday, to be the very embodiment of delectable chocolate nuttiness, her favourite combination. She was not disappointed.

ingredients

for the base:

200g/7oz plain (semisweet) chocolate-covered
   digestive biscuits or graham crackers

4 tablespoons butter, melted

2 tablespoons cocoa powder (unsweetened cocoa)

for the filling:

250g/9oz luxury plain (semisweet) chocolate

450g/2 cups cream cheese

280g/1 1/4 cups mascarpone cheese

2 teaspoons pure vanilla essence (extract)

200g/1 cup caster (superfine) sugar

2 organic eggs

for the candied pecan topping:

150g/1 1/4 cups pecan halves

2 tablespoons sugar

50g/2oz luxury plain (semisweet) chocolate

method

Preheat the oven to 180°C/350°F/Gas 4. Crush the chocolate biscuits or graham crackers in the food processor. Mix with the melted butter and cocoa powder, then press into the bottom of a 24cm/9½in cake tin (pan) with a removable base. Pack it down firmly with your fingertips or smooth down with the back of a spoon. Bake the base in the oven for 10 minutes, then remove and leave to cool. Lower the oven temperature to 160°C/325°F/Gas 3.

Melt the chocolate in a bowl set over a saucepan of simmering water. Alternatively, melt the chocolate in the microwave. To make the filling, whip the 2 cheeses together until smooth. Add the vanilla essence (extract) and sugar, and finally the eggs one at a time. Pour half the mixture into the cake tin (pan). Add the melted chocolate to the remaining mixture and stir until smooth. The chocolate mixture will be considerably thicker than the vanilla one. Spoon into the cake tin (pan) in patches over the vanilla mixture, then, using a sharp knife, swirl the 2 mixtures together by drawing several zig-zag patterns through the mixture. Bake in the oven for 30–40 minutes, until just set. If it wobbles slightly, remember that chilling will set it further.

Leave the cake to cool in its tin (pan) on a wire rack, then leave to chill for at least 3 hours or overnight. Meanwhile, make the candied pecans. Place the pecans in a dry frying pan over a moderate heat. Sprinkle over the sugar and stir until the nuts are toasted and the sugar becomes sticky and caramelized. Leave to cool.

Run a knife around the edge of the cake, then unmould, leaving the base of the tin (pan) attached to it, otherwise you risk breaking up the crust. Place on a large serving plate. To finish, melt the chocolate, then sprinkle the candied pecans over the top of the cake. Drizzle melted chocolate over the top to fuse the pecans in place and leave to chill in the refrigerator until ready to serve. Allow to return to room temperature. Soak a sharp knife in hot water, dry and use immediately for cutting each slice. Indulge.

top tip

This cake can be made as a sweet canapé. Cook in a rectangular oven tin (baking pan), then chill and cut into tiny squares and separate them. Top each square with a caramelized pecan, then drizzle with chocolate.

at the last minute

high-speed recipes, with minimal shopping

Spontaneity delivers some of the most memorable and relaxed occasions. This chapter is for those unexpected times in life – when old friends blaze into town without warning, when the weather is so beautiful you just have to get some mates over after work to eat in the garden ... when you can't be bothered to shop, but have some hungry hangers-on to feed, and you don't want them to know you can't be bothered!

Alas, a delicious last-minute meal can't be "magicked" out of thin air, but it can be rustled up from a well-stocked kitchen. See The Entertainer's Bag of Tricks, page 11, and take the book with you food shopping and enjoy stocking up. If unexpected guests pop by, you can even just grab some of those tasty morsels from the cupboard and make a meal of it with some couscous and chickpeas dressed in lemon and olive oil.

Here are some super-quick ideas:

Spicy soba salad Cook soba noodles, drain and cool under cold running water. Make a dressing of sesame oil, soy sauce, chopped chilli and spring onions (scallions). Stir through the noodles and serve, with lime wedges.

Porcini polenta Make soft, instant polenta, according to the packet instructions, using water in which you have first soaked a good clutch of dried porcini (cèpes) mushrooms for 10 minutes. (Add the porcini too!) Stir in lots of butter and Parmesan at the end.

Fig & walnut pasta While the pasta cooks, fry some onions in olive oil until soft. Drain the pasta and stir in chopped dried figs, chopped walnuts, cubes of blue cheese and the fried onions.

Saffron aïoli platter Pound a garlic clove with coarse salt until smooth. Stir in 2 pinches of saffron threads soaked in 1 teaspoon of hot water, a squeeze of lemon and 3–4 heaped dessertspoons of mayonnaise. Serve with potatoes and steamed vegetables.

hot & sour noodle bowl with chilli oil vegan

Thick and toothsome udon noodles are available ready-cooked in vacuum packs, for the quickest soups and stir-fries. They're satisfyingly slurpy in this zingy broth, but you could also use dried ramen or egg noodles, adding them to the broth early on, to cook with the vegetables.

ingredients

serves 4–6

500g/1lb 2oz cut mixed vegetables from the refrigerator
    or freezer, such as broccoli, cabbage, cauliflower, peas,
    courgettes (zucchini)

6 tablespoons dark soy sauce

6 tablespoons lime juice or rice vinegar, or a mixture

2 tablespoons sugar

3cm/1¼in piece of fresh root ginger, finely
    grated

400g/14oz udon noodles or other cooked
    noodles

for the chilli oil:

1 fresh red chilli, coarsely chopped

1 garlic clove

½ teaspoon coarse sea salt

2 tablespoons sesame oil

method

Put a kettle on to boil while you make the chilli oil. Pound or purée the chilli, garlic and salt in a mortar or spice grinder. Whisk in the sesame oil, then set aside until required.

Pour 1 litre/4 cups of boiling water in a saucepan, add the vegetables and return to the boil, adding the soy sauce, lime juice or vinegar, sugar and ginger. Simmer until the vegetables are tender, then add the noodles. Cook for 1 minute, or long enough to warm the noodles through.

Divide the soup between individual bowls. Dribble the chilli oil over each bowl and serve immediately.

artichoke soufflé omelette

This seriously sexy omelette will make a big impression — especially since it can be whipped up almost effortlessly. Serve with a salad, or just basking in its own lone loveliness.

ingredients

serves 2–4

5 eggs, separated

2 whole eggs

125g/4½oz artichoke hearts in oil, drained and sliced

55g/½ cup freshly grated Parmesan cheese

10 fresh basil leaves, shredded

salt and freshly ground pepper to taste

1 tablespoon butter (approximately 15g/½oz)

2 tablespoons olive oil

method

Using a fork, lightly beat together the 5 egg yolks and the 2 whole eggs. Using an electric hand whisk, beat the egg whites until stiff, then fold the whites carefully into the yolks, keeping it light and airy. Fold in the artichokes, Parmesan, basil and seasoning, again taking care not to lose the fluffiness.

Heat the butter and olive oil in a wide non-stick frying pan over a moderate heat. Pour in the omelette mixture and cook for about 5 minutes, until golden and crisp underneath. Depending on the size of your frying pan, it may not be possible to flip the omelette with a spatula, so you can try this method: slide the omelette on to a large plate, discard any excess oil so as not to risk getting burned, then invert the frying pan over the top of the omelette and flip the plate and frying pan over. Remove the plate, and cook the omelette for a further 1–2 minutes only, until softly set. Slide on to a warm serving plate, cut into wedges and eat immediately.

practically instantaneous pasta sauces

Prepared and cooked in less time than it takes to boil your pasta, these fresh sauces will knock the socks off any shop-bought sauce. Don't forget that fresh pasta freezes beautifully, so you can always have it to hand.

lemon spinach sauce

ingredients

serves 4

pasta of your choice
4 tablespoons olive oil
2 garlic cloves, crushed
1 small, fresh red chilli, chopped, or 1/4 teaspoon dried chilli flakes
300g/10 1/2 oz fresh or frozen leaf spinach
salt and freshly ground black pepper
6 tablespoons Greek (strained plain) or thick and creamy yoghurt
juice of 1/2 lemon

method

Firstly, put a large saucepan of salted water on to boil for your pasta. While the pasta cooks, heat the olive oil in a wide frying pan and fry the garlic and chilli for 1 minute. Add the spinach leaves, season with a little salt and black pepper and stir. Cover the frying pan while the spinach wilts, about 2 minutes for fresh, 4 minutes for frozen. Take the pan off the heat and stir in the yoghurt and lemon juice. Cover and leave to stand for 1 minute, then stir into drained pasta.

fried tomatoes & hazelnut pesto

ingredients

serves 4

pasta of your choice
for the pesto
1/2 garlic clove
1 teaspoon coarse sea salt
1 teaspoon pink peppercorns
25g/1oz/scant 1/4 cup blanched hazelnuts
2 handfuls of fresh basil and parsley, coarsely chopped

3 tablespoons freshly grated Parmesan cheese
4 tablespoons olive oil
for the tomatoes
2 tablespoons olive oil
2 medium tomatoes, thickly sliced
2 teaspoons balsamic vinegar
a pinch of sugar
salt and freshly ground black pepper

method

Put a large saucepan of salted water on to boil for your pasta. Meanwhile, make the pesto. Place the garlic, coarse salt and peppercorns in a mortar and pound to a paste with a pestle. Add the nuts and pound a bit, then add the herbs and grated Parmesan. Pound and grind until a coarse paste results. Add the olive oil and stir until incorporated. While the pasta cooks, heat the oil for the tomatoes in a wide frying pan over a moderate heat. Add the sliced tomatoes, vinegar and a little sugar and fry until slightly coloured on both sides. Season with a little salt and pepper.

Drain your pasta, though not too well, keeping it moist, then return to the saucepan. Scrape all the pesto into the pasta and stir vigorously to incorporate evenly. Serve topped with fried tomatoes.

an impromptu supper — Here's the strategy for the menu opposite: the Kerala-style Egg Curry (page 113) takes no more than 30 minutes to make, including preparation. So, to keep your guests nibbling happily in the meantime, prepare some delicious toasted flatbread and luxury houmous.

Turn the oven on to 200°C/400°F/Gas 6. Cut the flatbread into triangles and place on an oven tray. Drizzle with olive oil and sprinkle over a few sesame seeds, if you like. Toast in the oven until crisp, approximately 7–10 minutes. Scoop the houmous onto a plate; taste and stir in a little lemon juice if you think it needs it. Sprinkle over some dried mint, a few drops of olive oil, and finish with a cluster of caperberries. Stand some of the flatbread crisps in the houmous. Place a few pickled beetroots in another bowl with a few cocktail sticks.

shopping   If you do have time to shop, fresh houmous is always better than canned. Serve crackers in lieu of flatbread. Canned houmous is just one of the ingredients included in The Entertainer's Bag of Tricks (page 11), which lists useful staples to keep in the kitchen for impromptu entertaining.

crockery   At the last minute, anything goes.

drinks   If your impromptu guests come expecting to be fed, it's fair to remind them to bring a bottle, or a few cans. Save washing up and serve lager from the can or bottle. Beer promotes cheeriness, is a successful appetite curber, and tastes great with spicy food.

the menu

houmous topped with dried mint, olive oil & caperberries *108*

pickled baby beetroots (beets)

turkish flatbread toasted with olive oil & sesame seeds *108*

kerala-style egg curry *113*

ice cream with hot toffee-brandy sauce *90*

wok-fried noodles singapore-style

It's the curry powder, pepper and flat rice noodles that make this Singapore-style, but it's flexible, depending upon what you have in stock. Stir-fries are quick to cook, but what's the use if you're shredding, chopping and mincing for half an hour? Prep is kept to an absolute minimum here.

ingredients

serves 4 (more than this will be too slow and unwieldy in the wok)

150g/5½oz flat rice noodles

500g/1lb 2oz mixed vegetables – whatever you have to hand from the refrigerator or freezer; no more than
   4–5 types, such as broccoli, courgette (zucchini), (bell) peppers, mushrooms, peas, cabbage

2 tablespoons mild curry powder

125ml/½ cup water

2 tablespoons soy sauce

1 teaspoon salt

2 teaspoons sugar

½ teaspoon ground black pepper

½ teaspoon dried chilli flakes

2 handfuls of cashew nuts (approximately 55g/scant ½ cup)

8 garlic cloves, peeled and left whole

4–6 tablespoons sunflower oil

method

Boil a generous amount of water. Place the noodles in a bowl and pour boiling water over them. Leave to stand for 2 minutes – no more – then drain. Rinse under cold running water. They should be just par-cooked.

Cut up the vegetables so that they are in similar size chunks. Place in a bowl and sprinkle the curry powder over them. Stir and set aside.

Mix together the water, soy sauce, salt, sugar, black pepper and chilli.

Heat the wok as hot as you can – do not add oil. Toss in the cashews and stir until they take on a little colour, then remove from the wok. Toss in the garlic cloves (still, no oil) and char them in the dry wok, shaking occasionally, until they are blackened. Now add the oil and, very quickly, the vegetables. Stir vigorously. (Add a little more oil if it seems dry.) Stir-fry for 1–2 minutes, then add the noodles, cashews and the sauce mixture. Stir-fry for 2–3 minutes, until the vegetables are crisp-tender, the liquid is reduced and the noodles are cooked through. Serve right away.

think ahead

Noodles are such good fast food, so keep a selection in stock.

top tip

A traditional steel wok with a round base is probably the most useful pan in the kitchen, if you're cooking on gas. On an electric hob (burner), you'll need a wok with a flat base. Large ones are best so you can really move the food around without sloshing over. Traditional steel woks are thin and get very hot indeed, which is the secret of quick wok cooking. If the wok really is searing hot, you may need a little extra oil, which is why I've given two quantities. Always heat the wok first without oil to prevent sticking.

bulgur wheat in a spiced tomato sauce

This one is easy, fast, filling, warming and cheap – the ideal quick-fix supper. Inspired by an Iranian dish called "haleem", which is a sort of thick, savoury porridge, it becomes ever thicker as it stands.

ingredients

serves 4

400g/14oz can chopped tomatoes

1 fresh chilli, sliced and de-seeded if large, or
   1/2 teaspoon chilli powder

2 plump garlic cloves

2 teaspoons ground cumin

1 teaspoon brown sugar

1/2 teaspoon wine vinegar

salt and freshly ground black pepper

150g/51/2oz/scant 1 cup bulgur wheat

1 tablespoon dried mint

2 pieces of cinnamon stick or cassia bark (optional)

to serve:

thick and creamy yoghurt

extra virgin olive oil

a little ground cumin or cinnamon, for sprinkling

fresh parsley leaves (optional)

method

Empty the can of tomatoes into a blender and save the can. Add the chilli, garlic, cumin, sugar, vinegar, salt and black pepper and purée until smooth. Pour into a saucepan.

Pour 2 cans full of water into the blender in order to rinse it out, and then empty out the water into the saucepan. This will ensure that every last drop of purée is used. Add the bulgur wheat, dried mint and cinnamon or cassia bark. Bring to the boil and simmer for 10–15 minutes, stirring frequently, until the bulgur is cooked. Taste for seasoning. Ladle into bowls and serve with a dollop of yoghurt, a dribble of olive oil, and a pinch or two of cumin or cinnamon on top of each bowl. Garnish with parsley leaves, if you have them.

kerala-style egg curry

"Curry" is a Westernized concept meaning "stewed in sauce", and some curries are cooked to develop flavour over many hours or even days. This dazzling dish from southern India takes no more than 30 minutes all-in.

ingredients

serves 4

4 eggs

4 tablespoons sunflower oil

2 teaspoons black mustard seeds

2 large onions, finely sliced (approximately 400g/14oz)

3–4 garlic cloves, sliced

4–5cm/1 1/2 –2in piece of fresh root ginger, peeled and chopped

4 fresh chillies, halved lengthways

2 teaspoons ground turmeric

2 teaspoons cumin seeds

3 tablespoons desiccated (dried) coconut

salt and freshly ground black pepper

4 plump vine tomatoes, chopped, or 400g/14 oz can chopped tomatoes

250ml/generous 1 cup yoghurt

fresh coriander (cilantro) leaves, to garnish (optional)

freshly cooked basmati rice, to serve

method

Place the eggs in a small saucepan and cover with cold water. Bring to the boil and simmer for 5 minutes. Drain, rinse under cold running water until cooled, then peel and set aside.

Heat the oil in a wok or a large frying pan until quite hot. Add the mustard seeds and when they start to pop, lower the heat slightly, add the onion and fry until soft and golden. Add the garlic, ginger, chillies, turmeric, cumin, coconut, salt and black pepper. Fry for a couple of minutes until fragrant, then add the tomatoes and eggs. Stir gently until heated through, then remove from the heat. Stir the yoghurt through the mixture, then cover and leave to stand for 2 minutes. Sprinkle with whole coriander (cilantro) leaves if using, and serve with the freshly cooked rice.

7

fire & ice

outdoor food – picnics, barbecues and bonfires

Where there's fire, there's often ice – if you're eating outdoors. You'll be some distance

from the fridge and cooker, and you'll be either warming yourself – or cooking – with fire, and icing down your drinks; or, in the case of a picnic, icing down your food. Whatever the case, food always tastes better in the fresh air.

Picnics Clever containers and cool storage are paramount. Seek out tins of all shapes and sizes to fit non-liquid foods snugly – metal stays cool longer than plastic as well as preventing squashing and leaking. Indian stainless steel "tiffin" tins and spice jars are ideal. Keep sandwich bags full of ice and "freezer dogs" ready-frozen to wedge in between your containers. A cool box with a fridge element, which plugs into your car's cigarette lighter, is the perfect modern picnic "basket". Make a checklist – don't forget plates, napkins, cups or glasses, and a corkscrew.

Barbecues My guess is that nine out of ten vegetarians will prefer a separate barbecue. If you only have one, and you're cooking meat on it, borrow another, or get a disposable barbecue. Once the coals are lit, it will take around thirty minutes before they're ready to cook on. Wait until the flames have subsided; the coals should appear ashen. They should still be too hot to get close to; long-handled tongs and a long fork are essential for turning and rearranging the food.

Bonfires Who said *al fresco* eating had to be a warm weather affair? One of life's most exhilarating experiences is eating a hot meal by a toasty bonfire in winter. Stick to one rich soup or stew, eaten out of a disposable cup with a disposable spoon, and sip mulled wine or hot cider. Discard empties into the fire and take your garbage home.

pressed tuscan sandwich vegan

This sandwich resembles its Tuscan sister, the famous "panzanella", a salad of bread marinated in garlic, tomato and peppery olive oil. Here, the process of pressing squeezes these gorgeous Mediterranean flavours through the bread, which, as well as making it delicious, creates a nice tidy package that is easy to eat on a picnic.

ingredients

serves 4

1 medium ciabatta
1 garlic clove
1 medium vine tomato, chopped
10 fine black olives, stoned
2 teaspoons capers in vinegar, drained
5–6 sun-dried tomatoes in oil, drained and
*   coarsely chopped*
a small handful of fresh basil leaves,
*   coarsely chopped*
a small handful of flat-leaf parsley leaves,
*   coarsely chopped*
3 tablespoons extra virgin olive oil
1 teaspoon red wine vinegar
a pinch of salt
freshly ground black pepper

method

Slice the ciabatta in half lengthways, then cut the garlic in half and rub all over the surface of the bread.

Place the remaining ingredients in a food processor or mortar and pulse or pound until blended to a coarse paste. Spread over one side of the bread and top with the other piece.

For the pressing, you can either tie the sandwich up with raffia or cotton string, which is very pretty, or slip it in a large plastic bag and roll up, which is easier and more practical.

Place a flat board or large book on top of the sandwich and weigh down with a heavy object – a bag of sugar, a heavy mortar or a large container of water all work well.

Leave the sandwich to squash flat for about 1 hour before packing in your cool box.

think ahead

This sandwich is best made not more than four hours before eating.

top tip

Don't forget to bring a board and bread knife for slicing if taking this on a picnic. Alternatively, before departing, slice the sandwich into four pieces, stack and tie with string or wrap in cling film (plastic wrap).

serve with

Cheese, salad.

lemony lentils with radishes vegan

The cooking time of all legumes is determined by how old they are, which is the one thing they never tell you on the packet. Puy lentils usually take about half an hour, so taste after that long – they should melt in the mouth, without being mushy. This nutritious but delicious salad tastes great on a picnic, either packed into a well-sealed container (such as the tiffin tin shown), or stuffed into a portable pitta. It also makes a tasty accompaniment to barbecue fare.

ingredients	serves 6–8
	250g/2¼ cups green lentils, ideally Puy lentils
	juice of 1 large lemon
	2 tablespoons olive oil
	salt and freshly ground black pepper
	1 teaspoon fresh ground cumin
	2 spring onions (scallions), sliced
	8 radishes, halved
	a handful of fresh parsley, chopped

method
Rinse the lentils in a sieve, then place in a small saucepan. Cover generously with water, bring to the boil and cook at a moderate boil, without salt, until tender. Meanwhile, mix together the lemon juice, olive oil, salt, black pepper, cumin and spring onions (scallions). When the lentils are tender, drain them and mix with the dressing while still hot. Leave to cool completely, stirring now and then. Mix in the halved radishes and chopped parsley. Ideally it should be served at ambient temperature.

think ahead
Can be made one day ahead, keeping radishes separate. Stir in radishes close to eating time.

top tip
Any lentil can be used in this recipe except red ones – they are too soft and lose their shape. Lentils do not have to be soaked overnight before cooking, but larger legumes, including split peas and mung beans, are safer to eat after soaking and cooking.

picnic wraps

The globalization of the tortilla has made "wraps" into the new sandwich. These fillings can also be enjoyed on their own as salads: sprinkle the chickpeas with extra parsley and pimenton; omit the cream cheese from the beetroot (beet).

chickpea, courgette (zucchini) & pimenton wraps

ingredients
2 tablespoons olive oil
2 small courgettes (zucchini), thinly sliced (approximately 150g/5¹/2oz)
2 garlic cloves, chopped
2 teaspoons pimenton (smoked paprika) or mild chilli powder
400g/14oz can chickpeas
a pinch of salt
a squeeze of lemon juice
a small handful of fresh parsley, coarsely chopped
4 tablespoons yoghurt
4 medium-sized flour tortillas (wraps)

method
Heat the olive oil and fry the courgettes (zucchini) until soft and golden. Add the garlic and, when golden and fragrant, add the pimenton. When it changes colour, add the chickpeas with a pinch of salt. Cook for about 2 minutes, so the chickpeas heat through and become infused with flavour, then remove from the heat. Squeeze lemon juice over them and tip into a bowl. When cooled slightly, stir in the parsley and yoghurt.

Take a tortilla and place a spoonful of the filling towards the bottom. Fold over the sides, then fold over the bottom and roll up tightly. Place on a plate, cover and leave to chill until ready to eat or transport to your outdoor destination. Slice in half on the diagonal before eating.

beetroot (beet), blue cheese & walnut wraps

ingredients
100g/3¹/2oz baby beetroot (beet) in sweet vinegar, drained and coarsely chopped
55g/¹/2 cup walnuts, coarsely chopped
150g/5¹/2oz blue cheese, such as Stilton or Roquefort, chopped or crumbled
2 heaped tablespoons cream cheese
freshly ground black pepper
45g/1¹/2oz baby spinach leaves, washed and trimmed
4 medium-sized flour tortillas (wraps)

method
Combine the beetroot (beet), walnuts, blue cheese, and cream cheese in a bowl. Grind in a little black pepper and mash together with the back of a spoon until evenly combined. Proceed as above for stuffing, adding a pile of spinach leaves to each wrap.

melting mushrooms

Soft, fleshy mushrooms oozing rich, dark juice and garlicky cheese — what more could you want? Serve them with bread, so you can mop up every last drop that runs out of them.

ingredients

serves 4

8 large, open-cap or portobello mushrooms, of roughly equal size

4 tablespoons vermouth or white wine

2 garlic cloves, chopped

2 teaspoons fresh thyme leaves

salt and freshly ground black pepper

100–125g/3½–4½oz Gruyère cheese, or other melting cheese, grated

extra virgin olive oil

fresh crusty bread, to serve

method

Preheat the barbecue. Cut the stem out of the mushrooms, then score with a knife over the gills, not cutting through to the other side. Choose pairs of equal size. Lay one of each pair gill-side up on a work surface, then season to taste with salt and black pepper. Add 1 tablespoon vermouth or white wine, followed by a little garlic and thyme, and finishing with grated cheese. Place another mushroom on top and drive a cocktail stick or skewer through from the top to secure together. Brush all over with olive oil (These can also be baked in a 200°C/400°F/Gas 6 oven for 20 minutes or until soft).

Cook over hot coals, turning carefully once, until very soft, juicy and melting inside. Serve with crusty bread.

grilled miso-glazed aubergines (eggplants) vegan

If you're not familiar with miso, it's a fermented soybean paste with a strong, salty flavour. There are many types, each with different characteristics; I prefer the lighter colours to the darker ones. Miso gives a lovely depth to this glaze, which could be used for other vegetables, or indeed anything you put on the barbie.

ingredients

serves 4
large aubergine (eggplant)
wooden skewers, soaked for 30 minutes

for the glaze:
2 tablespoons miso
1 garlic clove, coarsely chopped
1 tablespoon tomato paste
1 tablespoon lemon or lime juice
2 teaspoons dark brown sugar
2 tablespoons sunflower oil

method

Preheat the barbecue. Cut the aubergines (eggplants) into 1cm/½in thick discs and drive a pre-soaked wooden skewer through each piece.

To make the glaze, whizz all the ingredients together in a small blender or spice grinder. Alternatively, pound the garlic with the miso paste until crushed, then whisk in the remaining ingredients until emulsified.

When the coals are hot, brush the aubergines (eggplants) on both sides with the glaze and cook, turning frequently with tongs and basting regularly, until very tender. Serve immediately.

grilled shiitake & tofu skewers vegan

Tofu has been around for two millenia, during which time the Japanese in particular have evolved some amazing and sophisticated recipes with the stuff. The simple teriyaki-style marinade – salty soy sauce, sweet mirin and nutty shiitake liquor – is a long-standing winner. My "tofu mantra" is this: keep it in its Asian home.

ingredients

serves 4

24 small dried shiitake mushrooms

500g/1lb 2 oz fresh, firm tofu

wooden skewers, soaked for 30 minutes

8 shallots, peeled

4 tablespoons dark soy sauce

4 tablespoons mirin (Japanese cooking wine) or sherry

sesame oil

method

Place the dried shiitake mushrooms in a bowl or large measuring jug and pour 150ml/^{2}/3 cup boiling water over them. Leave to soften for 20 minutes, stirring now and then. Meanwhile, drain the tofu and pat dry with kitchen paper (paper towels). Cut into 16 chunks.

Pick out the softened mushrooms and set the liquor aside. Thread the mushrooms and tofu on to 8 pre-soaked wooden skewers, with 2 pieces of tofu nestled between 3 mushrooms. Finish with a shallot on the end. Place the skewers in a container without stacking, so they can absorb the marinade.

For the marinade, stir together the soy sauce and mirin plus 4 tablespoons of the reserved mushroom liquor. Pour over the skewers and leave to marinate in the refrigerator for at least 1–2 hours. Turn the skewers over from time to time so they absorb the marinade evenly.

When ready to cook, brush the skewers with sesame oil. Cook over hot coals, or on a ridged griddle (grill) pan, turning over with tongs, until lightly charred on all sides.

think ahead Skewers can be prepared up to the cooking stage 1 day in advance.

top tip Don't use "silken" tofu – it won't hold together. Very fresh tofu can be bought at Asian food shops and health food shops. Try using tofu which has been frozen and thawed: it changes completely, taking on an amazing fibrous texture.

serve with Grilled Miso-glazed Aubergines (Eggplants) (page 123).

a bonfire party — The bonfire brings out the pagan reveller in us. "Bonfire Night" in Britain (November 5th) is an excellent excuse to celebrate our defiance of winter, whilst feasting, imbibing and watching fireworks. In the US, "tailgate parties" started as a gathering of football fans, beer and fire, and have evolved into thoroughly gourmet affairs embracing the same principle of enjoying the warm huddle while sharing food and drink, whatever the occasion and any time of year.

Before you consider hosting a bonfire party, you should obtain permission and advice to build a fire; consult your local fire department. They can offer advice and guidance on where and how to construct a safe fire. Use your common sense and never abandon a lit fire.

shopping   Army surplus stores often have a good selection of camping goods which might come in handy (thermoses, outdoor candles, flares, etc.).

crockery   This is one occasion for strictly disposable ware, ideally sturdy paper, which burns up in an eco-friendly fashion. Do not, however, burn polystyrene or plastic.

drinks   To make mulled wine, buy plenty of cheap and cheerful plonk. Make an infusion of 1 bottle of wine with cinnamon sticks, cardamom pods, and an orange stuck with cloves in a large preserving pan. Simmer for half an hour, then pour in more wine and heat until hot — not boiling, or the alcohol evaporates. Fortify with brandy and add sugar, if desired.

the menu

parsnip & coconut soup vegan

The clever thing about this soup is that it is thick. This means it won't slosh onto woolly coats, and it stays hot while you watch fireworks and have steamy-breathed conversations outdoors by the fire. It's rich and warming too; a meal in itself.

ingredients

serves 8–10

55g/4 tablespoons butter (vegans: use oil)
1 large onion, chopped
3 celery stalks with leaves, chopped
500g/1lb 2oz parsnips, coarsely chopped
300g/10½oz carrots, coarsely chopped
3 plump garlic cloves, chopped
1 tablespoon, plus 1 teaspoon ground cumin
salt and freshly ground black pepper
150g/5½oz block of creamed coconut, chopped
1 litre/1¾ pints/4 cups strong vegetable stock
a squeeze of lemon
Sweetcorn (Corn) Salsa, to serve

method

Melt the butter in a large saucepan, add the onion and cook until soft and translucent. Add the celery, parsnips, carrots, garlic, cumin, and season to taste with salt and black pepper. Stir, cover and leave to sweat, giving it an occasional stir, for about 10 minutes.

Meanwhile, place the chopped creamed coconut in a large bowl and pour 500ml/2 cups boiling water over. Leave for a few minutes, then stir until dissolved. Pour the coconut milk and vegetable stock into the saucepan and bring to the boil. Lower the heat to a simmer and cook until the vegetables are very soft, about 15 minutes. Leave to cool briefly, and then purée until absolutely smooth. Add a squeeze of lemon juice, purée again, then taste for seasoning. Serve on its own, or with Sweetcorn (Corn) Salsa.

sweetcorn (corn) salsa vegan — Spicy, crisp and juicy, this is the perfect garnish for the velvety soup.

ingredients

150g/scant ¾ cup sweetcorn (corn) kernels, blanched if fresh, or from a can, drained; 2cm/¾in piece of fresh red chilli, de-seeded and finely chopped; 1 spring onion (scallion), finely chopped; a few coriander (cilantro) leaves, chopped; a pinch of salt; 1 teaspoon lemon juice; 1 tablespoon olive oil

method

Combine all the ingredients in a bowl and serve a small amount on top of the Parsnip & Coconut Soup.

oven-roasted hot pot vegan

This richly warming dish requires minimal preparation. It's one of those genuine "whack it all in the oven" kind of recipes. The choice of vegetables is entirely flexible. Mushrooms and tomatoes are good because they're juicy; the rest can be any choice of seasonal veg up to about a kilo (2lbs) in weight. A tin of beans of some sort adds flavour and protein.

ingredients

100g/3½oz shiitake mushrooms
200g/7oz tomatoes
250g/9oz celeriac (celery root)
250g/9oz sweet potato
2 red onions
1 red (bell) pepper
100g/3½oz runner (string) beans
400g/14oz can chickpeas, drained and rinsed
4 garlic cloves, chopped

finely grated zest of 1 lemon
a handful of chopped fresh basil and parsley
1 teaspoon coriander seeds, crushed
a good grinding of nutmeg
salt and freshly ground black pepper
cayenne pepper to taste
1 litre/4 cups carrot juice, fresh or long-life
to serve (optional):
thick plain yoghurt
chopped fresh herbs

method

Preheat the oven to 180°C/350°F/Gas 4. Cut up all the vegetables into chunky bite-sized pieces and place in a deep roasting or casserole dish. Sprinkle over the rest of the ingredients and pour in the juice. Stir, then cover with foil and bake in the preheated oven for 45 minutes. Remove the foil and stir again. Lower the oven temperature to 150°C/300°F/Gas 2 and bake uncovered for a further 30–40 minutes to let the juices thicken.

Serve from the dish into warmed bowls. Garnish with a dollop of yoghurt and some more chopped herbs, if desired.

think ahead

Although this can be cooked in advance, there's something so appetizing about the cooking smells wafting out of the oven — it's part of the enjoyment of the dish.

top tip

If guests are standing, serve the hot pot in mugs or teacups.

serve with

Couscous, bulgur wheat, rice, quinoa or even baked potatoes. Lovely with Mustard Garlic Bread.

mustard garlic bread — This delicious diversion from the norm is always a hit. Cook it in the oven, on the barbecue, or in the embers of the bonfire.

ingredients

100g/scant 1 stick butter, softened (vegans: use margarine); 1 large garlic clove, crushed; 1 tablespoon coarse-grain mustard; freshly ground black pepper; 1 long French baguette, (approximately 75cm/29in)

method

Preheat the oven to 200°C/400°F/Gas 6. Beat together the butter, garlic, mustard and black pepper. Cut the bread into 1cm/½in slices, but do not slice all the way through the bottom. If it is too long to fit in the oven, cut into 2 pieces. Spread the butter mixture generously in between each slice. Wrap the bread up tightly in foil and bake in the preheated oven for about 15–20 minutes, until thoroughly heated through and slightly crispy. Serve immediately.

8

brunch

easy dishes that taste great early in the day

Brunch, a fusion of breakfast and lunch, is, not surprisingly, an American concept,

where it occupies a traditional slot at Easter and Mother's Day. Served any time between 10am and noon, it can also be the party-a-day-after-the-party, usually Sunday. The hair of the dog might be required – Bloody Marys, buck's fizz or mimosas are the order of the day.

When lots of people get together for a wedding or a big event, there is often a sequence of gatherings, culminating in a grand finale. Brunch bridges the gap between that finale and returning to normal life. It squeezes out that last bit of feasting, and provides an opportunity for a relaxed post-mortem of the previous night's event.

Brunch should be languorous and unfussy. No matter how few guests, brunch is a buffet – one course of many things, sweet and savoury, available for refilling over and over if desired. Always provide fruit, especially melons and berries, pots of coffee, juice, newspapers, and in the spirit of celebration, bubbly.

turmeric potatoes with lemon & coconut

For me, crispy potatoes take the prize for the tastiest morning food. Turmeric essentially dyes these potatoes a blinding yellow, while imparting a faintly earthy note in the flavour. The turmeric water turns an alarming blood red as it boils – this is OK! It's just doing its job.

ingredients

serves 6–8

1kg/2lb 4oz new potatoes, washed and halved

salt and freshly ground black pepper

2 teaspoons ground turmeric

3 tablespoons olive oil

6 garlic cloves

6 shallots, peeled

1 green (bell) pepper, chopped

1 lemon, thickly sliced

3 tablespoons unsweetened desiccated (dried) coconut

method

Preheat the oven to 220°C/425°F/Gas 7. Place the potatoes in a saucepan, cover with plenty of water and add a generous amount of salt and the turmeric. Bring to the boil and par-cook for 5 minutes. Drain thoroughly, and leave to cool slightly. Transfer them to a roasting dish and pour over the olive oil. Add the remaining ingredients and toss gently with your hands, ensuring everything is coated with a light slick of oil.

Roast in the preheated oven for about 30 minutes, stirring and dislodging sticky bits, until everything is thoroughly soft and crispy in places. Serve hot.

morning quesadillas with hot red sauce

"Quesadilla" is quite a loose term describing a Mexican-style fried tortilla encasing melted cheese, usually combined with beans, meat or vegetables. It's usually served as a snack, but also loves the company of eggs – yummy for breakfast. This simple oven-baked version, though far from traditional, is handy to make in quantity.

ingredients

serves 2–4
for the hot red sauce
400g/14oz can chopped tomatoes
2 small garlic cloves, crushed
a few slices of pickled jalapeño chillies
1 tablespoon jalapeño chilli juice from the jar
1–2 teaspoons mild chilli powder
salt
a pinch of sugar
for each quesadilla, you will need
olive oil
1 flour tortilla (wrap)
3 heaped tablespoons refried beans from a can
2 tablespoons cream cheese
1 spring onion (scallion), chopped
a little butter or olive oil, for frying
1 organic egg

method

Place the sauce ingredients in a small saucepan and bring to the boil. Simmer very gently while you cook the quesadillas.

Preheat the oven to 200°C/400°F/Gas 6. Spread the beans on one half of the tortilla and the cream cheese over the other half. Sprinkle with spring onions (scallions) and fold over. Brush generously all over with olive oil and place on a baking sheet. Repeat with the remaining tortillas. Bake in the preheated oven for 10–15 minutes, flipping once, until golden brown and hot throughout.

Meanwhile, heat a little butter or olive oil in a frying pan and fry the eggs until cooked to your liking. Serve the quesadillas with a fried egg and a little hot red sauce spooned over the top or in a dish on the side.

think ahead

The tortillas can be filled up to 4 hours in advance. Cover and keep in the refrigerator. The sauce can be made the day before and refrigerated.

top tip

If serving as part of a buffet, each quesadilla can be cut in half with a pizza cutter or knife to make smaller portions. Serve the hot red sauce in a separate bowl.

pine nut flatbread vegan

Flatbread makes a sassy alternative to toast. If you make the dough the night before, the pine nuts soften, forming little "stained glass" windows in the bread. Give it a whirl – it's dead simple, yet stunningly good.

ingredients

approximately 500g/3½ cups strong bread flour, plus extra for dusting

7g packet (approximately ¼oz package) easy-blend (active dry) yeast

2 teaspoons fennel seeds

2 teaspoons coriander seeds

3–4 tablespoons pine nuts

1 teaspoon salt

2 tablespoons honey (vegans: use brown sugar or malt extract)

method

Mix all the dry ingredients together in a large bowl. Dissolve the honey in 300ml/1¼ cups warm water, then add the water to the bowl gradually to form a soft dough. Add more flour if it's unmanageably sticky, but it should be just workable, not too stiff. Place the dough on your clean work surface (I use my kitchen table for breadmaking) and knead for about 5–6 minutes, until springy and elastic. Transfer to an oiled bowl and turn the dough in the oil. Cover the bowl and leave in a warm place until doubled in size. Alternatively, place in the refrigerator and leave to rise slowly overnight.

Preheat the oven to 220°C/450°F/Gas 7. Sprinkle flour over your clean, dry work surface. Gently punch the air out of the dough. Divide the dough into 8 pieces and roll out with a rolling pin into flat oval shapes. Irregular shapes are beautiful. Place the flatbreads on a baking stone or oven tray and cook in the preheated oven for 6–8 minutes, until golden and slightly puffed. (If you have an Aga or large flat griddle, you can cook the bread directly on the hot plate.)

wholewheat cheese pancakes

These light and healthy pancakes require so little effort, I often make them for breakfast half asleep, but they're good enough for entertaining, too. A tart fruit conserve is best with these, but they don't mind a little maple syrup either.

ingredients

serves 2–4

60g/scant ¹/₂ cup wholemeal (whole-wheat) flour

¹/₂ teaspoon baking powder

2 teaspoons light brown sugar

¹/₂ teaspoon salt

2 eggs, beaten

250g/generous 1 cup cottage cheese

¹/₂–1 teaspoon butter, for frying

method

Combine all the dry ingredients in a bowl and stir in the eggs and cottage cheese. Heat a heavy frying pan or griddle until moderately hot and add a tiny bit of butter, swirling it around to coat the surface. Cook heaped tablespoons of batter until slightly dry and bubbly on top, then flip over and cook until golden. Serve hot with yoghurt and cherry conserve.

think ahead

The batter can be made, omitting the baking powder, 12 hours in advance. Add the baking powder just before cooking. The pancakes can be cooked one hour in advance and kept warm, though they are best cooked fresh – leftover pancakes are, however, delicious reheated.

top tip

Cottage cheese usually has a plastic or foil covering under the lid – leave it in place after opening and it will keep longer.

a late morning buffet — The morning after a long night's sleep, particularly after a long night's partying, leaves most people with cravings, either for sweet things, or for a full savoury refuelling. Eggs, potatoes, fruit and pastries are the cornerstones of brunch. Individual espressos or cooked-to-order food have no place in this laid-back, grazing affair.

A note about eggs: the most important food to buy organic, if there had to be only one, is eggs. Compared to cheap battery eggs, organic eggs taste loads better — they have a richer, buttery yolk and a soft creamy white. The chickens have been reared to maximize their well-being; not to maximize egg production. They are able to roam free and are fed a natural, medication- and additive-free, vegetarian diet.

shopping	Morning gatherings will be much easier if the shopping, and much of the food preparation, has been done the day before. However, a sudden surge in numbers might warrant a trip to a bakery for some croissants or pastries.
crockery	Warm up large dinner plates in the oven for the savouries, and offer smaller cold plates for fruit and sweets.
drinks	On a hot day, make iced coffee. Firstly, brew a triple-strength pot of coffee. For those who take sugar, pour out half and sweeten with sugar while hot. Fill two jugs (pitchers) with ice and pour hot, sweet coffee into one, unsweetened into another. The ice will melt and dilute the extra strong coffee, while chilling it. Top up with milk. Make more for those who like it black.

the menu

banana, coconut & lime muffins

Let's face it – muffins are just a crafty excuse for eating cake for breakfast. As with all good cakes, the secret is to avoid overmixing. Don't worry if there are patches of unmixed flour in the batter, they will sort themselves out.

ingredients

makes 6 large muffins or 12 small ones

70g/generous ½ stick butter, melted, plus extra
  for greasing, or 90ml/⅓ cup sunflower oil

250g/scant 2 cups plain (all-purpose) flour

1 teaspoon baking powder

¼ teaspoon fine sea salt

200g/1 cup caster (superfine) sugar

2 eggs

grated zest and juice of 2 limes

1 teaspoon pure vanilla essence (extract) or
  1 tablespoon rum

125ml/½ cup yoghurt

1 large ripe banana, mashed

3 tablespoons unsweetened desiccated (dried) coconut

method

Preheat the oven to 180°C/350°F/Gas 4 and grease a muffin tin. Sift the flour, baking powder and salt into a bowl. Beat together the remaining ingredients in a separate bowl, then fold in the flour mixture in a few swift strokes, until barely combined, and still lumpy. Spoon into the greased muffin tin and bake in the preheated oven for 25–35 minutes, until golden, firm and springy to the touch.

Leave to cool in the tin for 10 minutes, then turn out onto a wire rack. Eat hot with butter.

apple marzipan muffins — deliciously fruity with a knockout almond flavour.

ingredients

Omit the lime zest and juice, banana and coconut and substitute *zest and juice of 1 lemon; 1 cooking apple or large tart apple, peeled, cored and diced; 100g/3½oz marzipan, cut into 5mm/¼in dice*

method

Proceed as for previous recipe.

eggs baked in tomatoes

This idea first came to me in a dream. I made it for breakfast that morning, and it was gorgeous. A few days later, I was flicking through a newly acquired copy of Margaret Costa's *Four Seasons Cookbook*, a timeless book first published in 1970. In it, I found Margaret's Eggs Baked in Tomatoes. She recommends them as a summer starter, and she adorns them with lashings of garlic, cream and bread fried in olive oil, which I'm sure could only make them even tastier if you're in that kind of mood. Still, the great collective cookery consciousness works in mysterious ways.

ingredients serves 4, or 8 as part of a brunch buffet
8 plump vine tomatoes
4 tablespoons olive oil
salt and freshly ground black pepper
8 fresh basil leaves
8 small to medium organic eggs
4 tablespoons freshly grated Parmesan cheese

method Preheat the oven to 200°C/400°F/Gas 6. Slice a tiny piece off the bottom of the tomatoes so they don't wobble, then slice off the top of the tomatoes and scoop out the cores, taking care not to pierce the shells. Place the tomatoes on a lightly oiled baking sheet and season the insides of the tomatoes with salt and black pepper. Lay a basil leaf inside and drizzle with olive oil. Break an egg into a teacup or small glass, then carefully pour the yolk into a tomato, leaving much of the white behind (discard extra). Repeat with all the eggs. Sprinkle grated Parmesan on top and bake in the preheated oven for 15–20 minutes, until set to your liking. Serve immediately.

think ahead The tomatoes can be hollowed out four hours in advance, wrapped in cling film (plastic wrap) and kept in the refrigerator.
top tip If plump vine tomatoes aren't available, use beef (beefsteak) tomatoes. Cut in half equatorially, scoop out cores and proceed with the recipe. If serving as part of a brunch buffet, place each tomato on a round of buttered baguette toast.
serve with Buttered toast.

9

when they eat fish

simple fish and seafood recipes for "pescetarians"

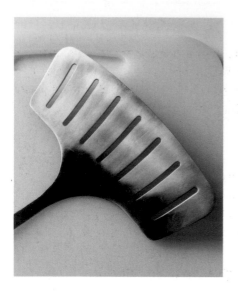
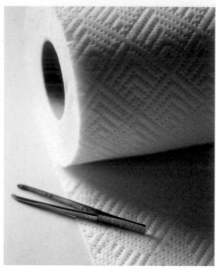

The concept of fish-eating vegetarians

may seem contradictory, but the fact is, they are a growing population. While everyone has their personal reasons for restricting their diet, the morality issues are not always the strongest. Often it's just a matter of taste.

So, this chapter is for the fish lovers!

Freshness, of course, is absolutely paramount with fish, perhaps more than any other food. Here are some guidelines on how to choose the best:

Go to a fishmonger (fish merchant), not a supermarket – it's likely to be fresher, cheaper and cleaner.

Don't shop for fish on Monday – it may have been caught on Saturday, or even Friday.

Ask questions. What's good today? Where's it from? If the fishmonger knows his or her stuff, there's plenty of interesting information to glean. Don't hesitate to ask for your fish to be completely prepared for cooking (cleaned, filleted, etc.) – that's the fishmonger's job, not yours. Save yourself the hassle. Fresh fish should look as though it's still alive and about to swim away. The eyes of the fish give a good indication of freshness. They should be clear, bright and bulging, not cloudy or withered. Look for sparkle!

Trust your nose. If the fish smells of anything other than the sea, reject it.

For this chapter, I have selected sustainable types of fish and seafood. However, this is unlikely to apply in every corner of the world, or forever. People who are concerned about these issues must make their own educated decisions. There are many helpful websites that offer information on this subject; two of the more useful ones are:

The Marine Conservation Society at www.mcsuk.org and the Monterey Bay Aquarium at www.montereybayaquarium.org.

chilli crab cakes with fresh sweet chilli dip

Fresh is always best, but frozen crab is perfectly acceptable for this recipe, and is likely to be cheaper than fresh. Get white meat only if possible, as brown meat can taste unappealingly gamey, and has a rather mealy texture. I have never been able to find crab available in any weight less than a pound, (450–500g), so this recipe uses it all up, and makes a lot of crab cakes. Many types of crab are overfished – choose snow crab, Dungeness or king crab.

ingredients

makes about 24, serves 8 as a appetizer

55g/2oz cream crackers or saltines, finely crushed

500g/1lb 2oz white crabmeat, thawed if frozen,
   squeezed dry and picked through

2–3 fresh red chillies, chopped

1 tablespoon Thai fish sauce, or light soy sauce

a handful of fresh coriander (cilantro), chopped

juice of 1 lime

1 plump garlic clove, chopped

1 organic egg, beaten

sunflower oil, for frying

lime wedges, to serve

for the dip:

75ml/⅓ cup golden syrup or light corn syrup

1 tablespoon light soy sauce

1 tablespoon lime juice

2 tiny spring onions (scallions), finely sliced

1 large fresh red chilli, chopped, or 2 small fresh red
   chillies, finely sliced

method

To make the dip, stir all the dip ingredients together in a bowl until thoroughly combined, then set aside.

Whizz the crackers in a food processor until they are a crumbly powder. Add the remaining ingredients and pulse until evenly and thoroughly combined, though not smooth. Form into 3–4cm/1¼–1½in wide cakes, no more than 1cm/½in thick.

Heat a shallow pool of oil in a wide frying pan over a moderate heat, until a tiny bit of the mixture sizzles immediately. Add the crab cakes and fry until golden and crispy on both sides, then drain. Serve with lime wedges and dip.

slow-cooked fennel & squid with pink peppercorns

The general rule with cooking squid is: cook it under two minutes or over twenty minutes. In between is the unappetizing rubber-band zone. Always get your fishmonger (fish merchant) to clean the squid for you, unless you fancy an icky lesson in cephalopod anatomy.

ingredients

serves 4

4 tablespoons butter (approximately 55g/2oz)

2 tablespoons olive oil

1 large fennel bulb (approximately 250g/9oz), trimmed and cut from head to base into wedges

250g/9oz squid, cleaned and cut into 1cm/½in rings

1 tablespoon pink peppercorns

salt

80ml/⅓ cup Madeira wine

2 heaped tablespoons breadcrumbs

400g/14oz pak choi (bok choy) or other leafy green vegetable, cleaned

1 tablespoon chopped fresh flat-leaf parsley

method

Melt the butter with the oil, which should stop it burning, in a large, heavy-based frying pan over a moderate heat. Add the fennel and squid and cook, stirring frequently, for 15 minutes.

Add the pink peppercorns, a good few pinches of salt, then pour in the Madeira wine. Cook until the wine reduces, then add the breadcrumbs and cook for a further 10 minutes, stirring frequently, so the fennel and squid get a good golden colour, and the breadcrumbs fry to a crisp. Meanwhile put the pak choi (bok choy) in a steamer and cook for about 5 minutes, until tender. Just before removing the squid from the heat, stir in the parsley. Serve on a bed of pak choi (bok choy), with any pan juices dribbled on top.

halibut with a warm tomato & basil vinaigrette

Flat fish like sole and halibut have a supremely delicate character. This warm, barely acidic vinaigrette lends itself well to feathery-textured fish. I cooked this for a wedding party of 130 people and it went down a storm.

ingredients

serves 4

4 tablespoons plain (all-purpose) flour

salt and freshly ground black pepper

500g/1lb 2oz halibut fillet, washed, left whole or
*   cut into 4 portions*

2–3 tablespoons olive oil

for the vinaigrette:

4 tablespoons olive oil

4 shallots, sliced

250g/9oz tomatoes, chopped

10–12 fresh basil leaves, chopped, plus extra to garnish

2 tablespoons red wine vinegar

1/2 teaspoon dark brown sugar

salt and freshly ground black pepper

method

Preheat the oven to 200°C/400°F/Gas 6. To make the vinaigrette, heat the olive oil in a small saucepan and add the shallots. Sauté until soft and translucent, then add the remaining ingredients. Cook until the tomato just starts to soften, about 2 minutes. Remove from the heat and set aside.

Sprinkle the flour on a plate and mix in a little salt and black pepper, then roll each fillet in the flour mixture. Heat the olive oil in a frying pan over a medium–high heat. Add the fish and fry on each side until lightly coloured, about 2 minutes per side, then remove the fish to a roasting tin (pan). (If your frying pan is ovenproof, place it directly in the oven.) Roast in the preheated oven for 8–10 minutes, until slightly shrunken, sizzling and cooked through. Serve immediately with the warm vinaigrette spooned over the top and a little extra chopped basil.

a thai-style feast —

Seafood is almost unavoidable in traditional Thai cooking — hardly surprising since Thailand is made up of thousands of islands. Like most Asian cuisines, it's built around creating a heightened sense of flavour through balancing the sweet, sour, hot and salty aspects of taste. A few exotic ingredients like tamarind, lemon grass and kaffir lime leaves give the cuisine its unique perfume. These ingredients may be difficult to acquire, but they freeze brilliantly, so stock up if you can.

Ornamental carved vegetables are a traditional garnish for Thai dishes on an everyday basis. Use fresh, smooth red chillies or spring onions (scallions). Hold the top firmly with your thumb and index finger, and slice several thin strips lengthways. Soak the spring onions (scallions) or chillies in a bowl of iced water for about thirty minutes to allow them to curl.

shopping   If you can't locate a shop specializing in South-East Asian produce, investigate mail-order shops on the Internet. These recipes don't require anything too obscure — fresh chillies, limes, mangoes and such should be easy to find. See notes on fish shopping at the beginning of this chapter. Note that the ice cream can be made without the kaffir lime leaves.

crockery   Thai food is traditionally eaten with forks, spoons and fingers, not chopsticks. If you can get fresh banana leaves, they make a gorgeous lining for plates and platters. Trim to size and sterilize by pressing into a very hot, dry frying pan. The leaf will turn bright green, and natural waxes in the leaf will come through to a brilliant shine.

drinks   Jasmine tea is the traditional drink with food in Thailand. Fruity white wine with a bit of sweetness is a good choice.

the menu

pappardelle with scallops, saffron & avocado

I will leave it up to you whether you want to leave the coral (roe) on the scallops — most pescetarians I've met prefer them without. This is a very subtly flavoured summer dish. I first cooked it when staying in a friend's beach house in Dorset; we got the scallops right off the boat from the diver himself. Strappy pappardelle carries the avocado-studded sauce nicely, but any long pasta will do. Make sure the water you cook the pasta in is as salty as the sea.

ingredients
serves 4 as a main course, 6 as a starter (appetizer)
12 scallops, cleaned and rinsed
sunflower oil
salt and freshly ground black pepper
2 tablespoons butter (approximately 25g/1oz)
4 shallots, finely chopped
1 red (bell) pepper, de-seeded and chopped into small dice
1 medium courgette (zucchini), chopped into small dice
1/4 teaspoon saffron strands, soaked in 2 teaspoons
   hot water
300ml/1 1/4 cups crème fraîche or soured cream
200g/7oz pappardelle
1 large perfectly ripe avocado, chopped chunky, and dressed in the
   juice of 1 lime

method
Place the drained scallops in a bowl and add just enough oil to barely coat them. Season lightly with salt and black pepper and leave to chill in the refrigerator.

Bring a large saucepan of well-salted water to the boil for the pasta.

Meanwhile, melt the butter in a large saucepan over a gentle heat. Add the shallots, red (bell) pepper and courgette (zucchini) and cook, stirring frequently, until the shallots are soft and golden. Add the saffron water, and stir in the crème fraîche or soured cream until heated through. Season with a little salt and black pepper, then remove from the heat, cover and set aside.

Cook the pasta for about 6–8 minutes, until al dente. (Alternatively, follow the packet instructions.) Heat a ridged griddle pan (grill pan) until very hot, for cooking the scallops. When the pasta has 4 more minutes cooking time, place the scallops on the hot pan and cook for 90 seconds on each side, turning over with tongs, then remove from the heat. Drain the pasta and return to the saucepan. Stir the saffron sauce and the chopped avocado through the pasta until evenly coated. Divide the pasta between 4 warm plates and top with the cooked scallops. Serve immediately.

think ahead
This dish is best prepared just before eating.

top tip
Opt for diver-caught scallops as dredging damages the sea bed. Although I got the scallops from the diver, I still took them along to the fishmonger (fish merchant) to have them expertly removed from the shell.

thai tuna & mango salad

Fresh tuna is one of the meatiest fish around, and it's always a good idea to ask people how they like their tuna cooked, just like a steak. Most tuna lovers prefer it pink, as it does have a tendency to get leathery if overcooked. When selecting your fresh tuna, make sure it is "dolphin friendly", and is not a bluefin tuna, which is an endangered species. Albacore tuna and yellowfin tuna are better choices, ideally if they are line-caught.

ingredients

serves 4

for the salad:

125g/4oz egg noodles

1 tablespoon sunflower oil

500g/1lb 2oz fresh tuna steak, cut into cubes

1 medium mango, peeled and cut into strips

1 red (bell) pepper, cut into thin strips

1 small red onion, finely sliced

a large handful of fresh mint, leaves stripped

a large handful of fresh coriander (cilantro), leaves stripped

for the dressing:

1 garlic clove, finely chopped

1 fresh red chilli, finely chopped

4 tablespoons light soy sauce

2 tablespoons Thai fish sauce or 2 extra tablespoons light soy sauce

4 tablespoons lime juice

2 tablespoons dark brown sugar

method

Boil the noodles for 5 minutes, or cook according to packet instructions. Drain, then rinse under cold water until cool. Place in a large bowl.

Whisk all the dressing ingredients together. Alternatively, whizz in a blender.

Heat the oil in a non-stick frying pan until very hot. Add the tuna and cook for a few seconds on each side until seared, or cooked to your liking.

Pour half the dressing over the noodles and toss to coat evenly. Arrange the noodles on 4 plates. In the bowl which contained the noodles, combine the tuna with the rest of the salad ingredients and the remaining dressing and toss until well coated. Spoon on top of the noodles and serve.

index

for Dad

acknowledgements

My most heartfelt thanks to the dynamic team — Vanessa, Jan and Nicky — sparks flew. Huge thanks to Stuart Cooper for keeping hold of the reins, and for believing in me throughout, and to Lizzy Gray for her sharp focus and massive patience. Now for all the people who helped make this book the entity it is, with love:

Christiane Kubrick, Anya and Jonathan, Amy, Beth and Mom, for your undying support

Suku, for auspicious friendship and the exquisite vegetable carvings, Emma, Andrew, Calum, Annette

Cathy Lowis

Tamsyn, Brent and Shannon

Vanessa's Luke and Rosie and Mandy's Rebecca and Tilley the cat

Jennifer Joyce, Victoria Blashford-Snell

Lindsay Wilson

Recipe tasters Paula, Tracy, Ben, Kate, Paulie, Ying, Jill, Matt, Roland, Selene, James, Jessica and little Sorrel (farther down the food chain), Rupert, Jeanne, and my lovely Dan

Rosie Kindersley and Eric Treuille and all the staff at Books for Cooks

Thanks also to: Lindy at Ceramica Blue — www.ceramicablue.co.uk; Camilla Schneideman at Divertimenti — www.divertimenti.co.uk; SCP — www.scp.co.uk; Little Book of Furniture — www.littlebookoffurniture.com; Aria — www.ariashop.co.uk; Patricia Michaelson at La Fromagerie — www.lafromagerie.co.uk; John Lewis Partnership; Renata at Giaccobazzi's; Steve Hatt fishmongers, Essex Road, London N1; James Elliot, Essex Road, London N1

First published in Great Britain in 2003 by Pavilion Books, 64 Brewery Road, London N7 9NT A member of **Chrysalis** Books plc
Text © 2003 Celia Brooks Brown   Photography © 2003 Jan Baldwin   Design © 2003 Pavilion Books

The moral rights of the author have been asserted.

Senior Commissioning Editor: Stuart Cooper   Editor: Lizzy Gray   Art director: Vanessa Courtier   Styling: Celia Brooks Brown   Styling Assistant: Nicki Hill

Printed and bound by Imago, Singapore. Cataloguing-in-publication Data: a catalogue record for this book is available from the British Library.   ISBN: 1-86205-534-3